SCARED WHEATLESS

MARY JO EUSTACE

SCARED WHEATLESS

DELICIOUS *gluten-free* RECIPES THAT WON'T MAKE YOU LOSE YOUR MIND

MARY JO EUSTACE

whitecap

Whitecap Books is known for its expertise in the cookbook market, and has produced some of the most innovative and familiar titles found in kitchens across North America. Visit our website at www.whitecap.ca.

EDITOR: Patrick Geraghty and Penny Hozy
DESIGN: Diane Robertson
COVER DESIGN: Andrew Bagatella
COVER PHOTO: Alexandra DeFurio
FOOD PHOTOGRAPHY: Tracey Kusiewicz
FOOD STYLING: Tracey Kusiewicz
PROOFREADER: Caroline Helbig

Library and Archives Canada Cataloguing in Publication

Eustace, Mary Jo, author
Scared Wheatless / Mary Jo Eustace.

ISBN 978-1-77050-244-4 (pbk.)

1. Gluten-free diet--Recipes. 2. Cookbooks I. Title.

RM237.86.E87 2015   641.5′638
C2014-908058-1

We acknowledge the financial support of the Government of Canada and the Province of British Columbia through the Book Publishing Tax Credit. *Nous reconnaissons l'appui financier du gouvernement du Canada et la province de la Colombie-Britannique par le Book Publishing Tax Credit.*

Canadä

15 16 17 18   5 4 3 2 1

PRINTED IN CHINA

This book is dedicated to the A Team—
Maureen, Michael, Jack, and Lola

And the Celestial One—Ken Kostick
June 1, 1953–April 21, 2011

CONTENTS

WELCOME TO MY NIGHTMARE...

I have been in the food business for over 20 years (obviously since I was a teenager!) and have been lucky enough to have created and starred in two hit food shows, with over 800 television episodes to my credit. Product endorsements, multiple cookbooks and media tours followed, with a little bit of personal drama thrown in for good measure. It has made for a very interesting life and career.

I have always loved food and creating recipes, and was more excited to go to school in Montreal for the culinary excellence than obtaining a degree. I've always found food to be the great equalizer—something everyone can relate to. I have educated aspiring chefs on everything from Greek yogurt to lemongrass to ginger, and the magic of a shot or two of English port. Traveling extensively across the country has also given me a real feel for what people have access to and can cook and execute on a daily basis. Sometimes they are super-inspired, Iron Chef-style, and sometimes it's easy to get a little lazy. I am a cookbook author and a supposed food expert for God's sake, but the big joke is, "Let's go over to Mary Jo's house for dinner! You know, the one where we have to bring our own?"

Look, I'm not proud of it. Life just got a little busy. Single mom, two kids, work, and with everything in between, who has the time to cook, especially if I can buy it ready-made, right? So that became my time-starved mantra—"I'll just buy it already packaged up." Is this starting to sound familiar to all of my fellow overextended moms (and dads) out there?

Then just when I thought I had it all under control, out of nowhere I got hit hard by the nutrition police. My daughter Lola was diagnosed with an autoimmune disease, alopecia areata, and her hair started falling out. I mean, what the hell is autoimmune disease and why did it show up at my door? Well, guess what? It showed up again a month later when I got cellulitis (a bacterial skin infection) from being rundown, and I had an allergic reaction to the drugs, which triggered an autoimmune reaction for me, too. All of a sudden I was in a bad movie (again) and I didn't like where this one was going.

So I started researching, reaching out, connecting, and talking to individuals, families, and other people who were suffering from autoimmune diseases, food intolerances, and dietary problems. I kept hearing the same thing again and again—avoiding gluten, eating clean, and getting rid of the crap in our diet seemed to be the common threads. Everywhere I went, every party, every event, someone had a story and it was always the same—it seemed to really matter what fuel we were putting into our bodies, and that many of us were running on empty.

Simply put, autoimmune diseases occur when the body's immune system (rather than foreign bacteria) attacks and destroys healthy body tissue by mistake. Autoimmune disease takes many forms and the exact cause is unknown. However, there are many triggers that confuse the immune system, such as environmental toxins, poor diet, stress, and processed, chemically-laden foods, which our bodies rebel against. Everyone, from Dr. Oz to Dr. Susan Blum to thousands in between, talks about the ability to eat ourselves healthy through the nutritional lifestyle choices we follow. And the number one step appears to be eliminating gluten from the diet. For people with celiac disease, eating gluten can be life threatening; for those with an intolerance, it can affect their health and well-being.

This is my story and my handbook on how to move toward healing. I am not a doctor—I don't even play one on TV—nor am I a nutritionist, but I am a pit bull of a mom who, when faced with a sick child, explored every option available. As a result of everything I was learning, I hired a nutritionist who works a lot with kids with dietary restrictions and autoimmune disorders, and she told me her practice had never seen so many unhealthy children as it had in the last couple of years. It makes sense—we ingest foods with ingredients we can't pronounce, huge companies are saturating the market with genetically modified foods, and sugar and sodium are in everything. Add to this the stresses of everyday life, where a family doesn't even have the time nor the financial resources to buy high quality, safe foods. Over time, if we fuel our bodies with less nutritious and chemically-laden food, we will eventually pay the price. Don't even get me started on global warming…

I know there are millions of people out there who have to do this "gluten-free," healthier eating thing. It can be intimidating and totally suck, and if one more person says "gluten-free" to you, you might just drop-kick their "gluten-free" ass to the curb. But I want this experience to be different. Google anything from "gluten-free" to "auto-immune" to "chronic fatigue" to "psoriasis" and you will find there is a revolution among doctors, health professionals, and nutritionists, who are embracing and promoting the necessity of healthy, conscientious eating for the well-being of ourselves and, most importantly, our children.

The purpose of this book is to give you easy, realistic recipes to incorporate gluten-free options and different food choices into your life. I will also provide alternatives in recipes to soy and dairy. And I promise you won't have to grind nuts for hours for a pie crust, or go into seclusion to avoid ever encountering gluten again!

I admit that I went into this thing kicking and screaming, terrified that it would consume my life and alienate Jack, my six-foot-four son who has to eat every three minutes…but it didn't! I actually started to care about the food we were putting into our bodies. My son thinks I make him separate meals that aren't gluten-free or healthier—he's even smug

about it. Just wait until he finds out he's been eating the same thing…

Nothing will bring you to your knees quicker than a child or loved one who has a health condition. That is where all this started, and I have become obsessed with making this journey easier for all of us on this health trajectory. We are a big group.

So get ready for a five-minute summary of autoimmune disease and gluten-free eating. Don't worry, it won't be too painful. My attention span isn't that long. But first, let's get caught up on a few things…

Thanks, autoimmune disease— could my life be any more complicated?

OUR REASON FOR GOING GLUTEN-FREE

It's funny in life how there are markers where your life can change so profoundly in the blink of an eye that everything following that moment is divided into "before" and "after." My marker is October 28, 2013, when I noticed my daughter's alopecia for the first time. Naturally it was on a Saturday night when the doctor's office was closed and I had a full 48 hours to Google every disease known to mankind, even self-diagnosing myself along the way with a few terminal ailments, just for good measure! I was terrified— all of a sudden my beautiful girl had a bald spot on the top of her head and another one over her left ear. I knew it was alopecia and it was confirmed Monday morning at the pediatrician's office. I had to ask them to tell me in a separate room because I couldn't stop crying. Next stop was the dermatologist—an old and crusty one who said there was nothing anybody could do. No prognosis, no cure—it could all go away, grow back, or not. It was an autoimmune response, possibly triggered by stress and would I like some ointment? Might be useless, but try it anyway and come see me in six months. How inspirational!

I felt totally helpless and powerless. We were expected to just sit around doing nothing and wait to see if all her hair fell out. I simply could not accept it. I started to reach out to other doctors, nutritionists, naturopaths, and friends who had similar experiences with autoimmune disease. One of the first things I did was find another doctor (duh!) and get a nutritionist on board after reading article upon article about people reversing or improving their autoimmune conditions through a clean, gluten-free diet. That made sense to me once I began to understand the pathology of autoimmune disorders.

Simply explained, autoimmune disease occurs when the body's immune system, which normally defends your body against disease, decides your healthy cells are foreign and attacks and destroys healthy body cells. This type of reaction can be triggered by harmful substances that include bacteria, viruses, toxins, and some drugs. Substances that stimulate a response by the immune system are called antigens. Antigens are molecules that may be contained within cells or on the surface of cells (such as bacteria or cancer cells) or be part of a virus.

The immune system, when it is working at an optimum level, produces antibodies against these antigens that enable it to destroy these harmful substances. But the cells that control antibody production—for example, B cells (a type of white blood cell)—occasionally malfunction and produce abnormal antibodies that attack some of the body's cells. When you have an autoimmune disorder, your immune system does not distinguish between healthy tissue and antigens. It is confused and, as a result, the body sets off a reaction that attacks healthy tissue and causes prolonged inflammation, creating all sorts of problems like lupus, rheumatoid arthritis, Hashimoto's disease, celiac disease, psoriasis, and fibromyalgia, just to name a few. In Lola's case, the autoimmune disease is attacking her hair follicles.

There has been no definitive word on what triggers alopecia—some theories that have been bounced around are that microorganisms (such as bacteria or viruses), genetics, or drugs (antibiotics, medications) might induce a reaction. Even stress is thought to be a possible factor.

So, if you are not totally asleep by now, you might ask yourself: "What does gluten have to do with all this s**t?" I'm glad you asked.

Here is the skinny on gluten: It is a general name for the proteins found in wheat, rye, barley, and triticale. Gluten helps foods hold their shape and it is the kick that gives dough its elasticity. It is found in tons of foods and products that you would never suspect—from soy sauce, to beer, to lots of salad dressings and marinades, all the way to corn chips that are mixed with wheat, and even your favorite granola bars and cereals. The good news is that it is easy to get a list of gluten-free foods (from Google) and most products say gluten-free right on the label. Gluten is difficult for many people to digest, and here is why.

Celiac disease, which is the most extreme case, is an autoimmune and digestive disorder that results in damage to the lining of the small intestine when foods containing gluten are eaten. The body can't process the gluten and instead the immune system forms antibodies to gluten that then attack the intestinal lining, causing inflammation and damage to the intestine, making it extremely difficult for the body to absorb many nutrients. This can lead to painful abdominal bloating, anemia, weight loss, joint pain, severe tiredness, osteoporosis, skin problems, and even malnutrition. It can also cause tearing in the intestinal lining, allowing all those nasty bacteria to leak into the body—a syndrome known as "leaky gut."

Here's the deal—you can be gluten sensitive without having celiac disease (or gluten antibodies) and still have inflammation and signs of autoimmune disease. You can also have similar symptoms—bloating, fatigue, diarrhea, inflammation of your joints, depression, and brain fog, and not be celiac, just gluten intolerant. I meet people on a daily basis who tell me their stories of reversing their health problems through a good gluten-free diet—whether they have celiac disease, chronic fatigue, hair loss, or joint pain.

And, as my nutritionist said, it is showing up more and more in our children. It seems to me that as our diet depends increasingly on processed foods, there are more cases of autoimmune disease showing up. We have already made one connection—celiac disease is a direct result of gluten and diet. That alone is a pretty compelling argument for diet affecting autoimmunity.

Even if you don't have any signs of autoimmune disorder and just feel sluggish after eating gluten, come along for the ride. It is estimated that about 5 to 6 percent of the population in the United States could be gluten sensitive—about 18 million people in all. Celiac disease affects about one in every 133 people. The gluten-free movement is increasing its momentum every day.

So I ask myself, what if this pesky gluten makes a little hole in the intestine or irritates and inflames, sending Lola's body into crazy mode? If I can alleviate it, fix it, make it better with a healthy diet—it's worth a shot. It stands to reason that with all the processed food in our diet, the toxins in the environment, and the constant stress in our lives, our bodies might just react in a negative way, get a little confused, and start screwing up badly.

It makes sense to me. We have been following a gluten-free lifestyle since November 15, 2013, and I am overjoyed to tell you my little girl's hair is growing back—"Houston! We have regrowth!" And just as important, a healthy, happy child who likes quinoa and broccoli soup. You know why? Because it tastes good…

One last thing, I promise!

THE DIFFERENCES BETWEEN BEING "WHEAT-FREE" AND "GLUTEN-FREE"

There are a few differences between wheat-free and gluten-free, but the most important fact to remember is that someone can be on a wheat-free diet and not be on a gluten-free diet. All wheat contains gluten, but gluten is also found in rye and barley. So, for instance, if you have an allergy to wheat, you can still eat things containing gluten as long as they are not wheat based. Make sense? But if you have an intolerance to gluten and an inability to digest it properly, then you have to stay away from all products with gluten. You will also notice when you start reading labels that many products come in contact with wheat in the factories where they are made. For someone with a serious wheat allergy, this can be life threatening.

I know I have given you a lot of information, but it all leads to my pantry chapter. There can be hidden triggers in some of the foods and sauces you are buying that might defeat all your efforts to be gluten-free. That is why it is essential to know what is in your foods—and starting now, we are so covering that!

GETTING YOUR PANTRY STARTED

MAKING YOUR PANTRY A PLACE YOU ACTUALLY USE

After years of cooking, cooking school, and writing cookbooks, the most important thing I have learned is that to rock it in the kitchen you have to rock it in the organizational department. Your kitchen and surrounding areas cannot be harder to navigate than *The Amazing Race*—you have to get your proverbial house in order, and even more so if you are cooking gluten-free. It all comes down to actually having the ingredients in your kitchen so you can use them unfettered, without scrambling around for things you need or that are missing. Great food and execution comes down to a very simple concept: knowing what you have and how to use it.

Now that you are cooking gluten-free, it is paramount that you have a well-stocked kitchen and pantry that facilitate your new attitude toward food and preparation. It is essential to have quality dry ingredients on-hand that you will supplement with fresh food and produce. We want this to be as simple as possible—we are getting rid of the gluten, and hopefully, like an obnoxious, cheating ex-husband, you won't miss it at all!

The key to your success lies in having the basics to make gluten-free sauces and staples along with the produce and protein to pair them up with. Once you get the hang of making your own sauces, salads, dressings, and dips, a few things will happen. First, you will become addicted to how delicious they taste and how easy they are to prepare, and second, you will learn how economical taking charge of your health and kitchen can be. We waste so much money on crap that we never end up using, and ingesting ingredients that are impossible to pronounce and even more difficult to digest and process. Once you have command of how you cook and flavor your food, you will become more creative, more discerning, and most certainly healthier.

MY THREE FAVORITE INGREDIENTS

Never underestimate the value of a great olive oil, high-quality sea salt, and cracked black pepper. I know you

Flavor Your Own Olive Oil

As I was almost out of the green lemon olive oil that I got on a summer fling in St. Tropez (don't ask—it ended badly), I decided to make my own. Take 5 or 6 lemons and peel the skin, making sure there is no flesh left on the peel! Allow the peel to dry for 2 to 3 hours. When completely dry, place the lemon peel in a Mason jar or bottle that can hold 3 cups (750 mL) of olive oil. Pour the olive oil over the lemon peel and seal the jar or bottle tightly. Store for 2 weeks in a dark place. When ready, strain the olive oil through a sieve and discard the lemon peels. Voila—lemon olive oil!

You can also add herbs but be sure anything you put in the olive oil is dried out with no moisture to prevent the potential for bacteria and mold!

Apple Cider Vinegar

This is the quinoa of the vinegar world and it has many nutritionists singing its praises. Made from pulverized apples and high in acetic acid, it can help your body absorb more of the minerals from the foods you eat. It also might help in regulating insulin and slowing down the absorption of sugar. There are lots of studies on apple cider vinegar's affects on blood pressure, diabetes, pH levels, and weight loss that put forth a compelling argument to use it on a regular basis.

have watched those cooking competition shows where the judges always say the same thing: "Don't forget to season your food!" It's true—you can prepare a great dish, but forget to season it and it turns out bland. That's okay for your accountant, but it's not okay for a recipe you have slaved over for hours. Tasting as you go along saves a lot of heartache in the end. It also connects you to what you are creating, which is important. You and your food are dating now—so mutual respect, understanding each other's needs, and separate bank accounts are a must!

OILS AND VINEGARS—A QUICK INTRODUCTION

Oils and vinegars are essential to great cooking, sauces, and salad dressings. Olive oil, sesame oil, grapeseed oil, walnut oil, canola oil, sunflower oil, and peanut oil all offer different benefits. Peanut oil is great for frying and in stir-fries because of its high smoking threshold (use sesame oil only for flavor). I will spend more for a great olive oil, especially for dressing salads or drizzling on lovely fresh heirloom tomatoes. The same goes for vinegars—experiment and see what you like. I am obsessed with rice wine vinegar and apple cider vinegar right now—I use them in everything.

What to put in your pantry!

Here are a couple of basic lists to help you stock your kitchen. The first list contains dry goods that don't need refrigeration (except for the pizza shells). The second list supplements the dry goods with fresh produce and other extras for great cooking.

PANTRY LIST

* Oils—olive, sesame, walnut, grapeseed, canola, peanut, sunflower, vegetable, toasted sesame, pumpkin seed

* Vinegars—apple cider, balsamic, red wine, rice wine, white, tarragon, etc.

* Quinoa

* Rice—basmati, jasmine, brown, sticky, risotto

* Tamari sauce (gluten-free) and fish sauce

* Garlic, fresh or minced in a jar

* Ginger and lemongrass, fresh or minced in a jar

* Chicken and vegetable stock (gluten-free)

* Coconut milk, canned

* Nuts and seeds—walnuts, pine nuts, pecans, cashews, pistachios, almonds, plus sunflower seeds, hemp seeds, chia seeds, flaxseed, coriander seeds, fennel seeds

* Polenta

* Beans, canned and dry—black beans, chickpeas, lentils, kidney beans, cannellini beans, pinto beans

* Dried fruit—apricots, cranberries, cherries, figs, dates, raisins, currants

* Dried herbs—basil, oregano, parsley, rosemary, thyme, marjoram, mint

* Spices—turmeric, cumin, curry powder, nutmeg, cinnamon, Chinese five-spice powder, saffron, paprika, chili flakes, allspice, cracked black pepper, sea salt, star anise

- Pasta (gluten-free)—quinoa, corn, rice-based noodles
- Bread—pizza shells (refrigerate), gluten-free bagels, breadcrumbs, wraps
- High-quality canned tomatoes
- Tuna and crab, canned
- Dijon and grainy mustard
- Olives
- Capers
- Sundried tomatoes, roasted red peppers
- Honey, brown sugar, maple syrup
- Crunchy organic peanut butter
- Canned pumpkin
- Curry paste, miso paste (gluten-free)
- Nutritional yeast (see sidebar)

FRESH PANTRY LIST

Buy items on this list on a bi-weekly or daily basis.

- Eggs
- Butter
- Greek yogurt
- Fresh herbs—basil, mint, thyme, cilantro, Italian parsley
- Almond or coconut milk
- Vegetables—broccoli, carrots, peppers, spring onions, mushrooms, bok choy, celery, butternut squash, pumpkin, parsnips, sweet potatoes, Yukon Gold potatoes
- Fruit—apples, pears, avocados, tomatoes, oranges, grapefruits, pineapples, mangoes, papayas
- High-quality Parmesan cheese

Nutritional Yeast

Nutritional yeast is one of my new favorite things (it is not brewer's yeast). It is gluten-free, low fat, and packed with nutrients. It has a delicious nutty, savory, cheesy taste and is great sprinkled on salads and soups, and divine on popcorn. It makes scrambled eggs more creamy—the same with mashed potatoes. Combine it with some ground pistachios or almonds and use as a crumble on top of baked vegetables. You will love it.

- High-quality feta and goat cheese
- Limes and lemons
- Mayonnaise
- Pancetta or bacon
- Fresh fish
- Organic boneless chicken breasts
- Ground pork or beef or turkey

These two lists combined give you a great start. I am very much in favor of buying produce, dairy, and meat as fresh as possible. It is also a great way to cut down on waste. That is how the Europeans and Asians do it—the quality not quantity of food is the most important thing. I am also going to let you in on another little secret that has saved my life many a time. Wait for it . . .

How I cut down my yelling on a weekly basis

I preplan. I know it is not hot and sexy to be thinking of my turkey burgers on a Saturday night, but I do. To reduce my already accelerated stress level (have I mentioned stress is not good for your health?), I do a few things on Sunday that make my hellish work/school week a whole lot nicer. I whip up a few sauces—maybe my **Asian Orange Sauce** (see p. 28) or a pesto or two—a basic salad dressing, and I cook up some pasta or quinoa. That's it.

I lovingly place the cooked items in my Ziploc bags, the dressings in Mason jars (my other reason for living), and I take a deep breath. I have two or three dinners ready to go and I start to calm down. For example—Monday night can be baked chicken with **Balsamic Mushroom Pesto** (see p. 22), arugula with my **Dijon Mustard Lemon Swirl** (see p. 13), and quinoa with fresh herbs and almonds.

Tuesday can be **Peanut Envy** (see p. 27) over cold noodles with cucumbers, peppers, and some tofu or shredded chicken or beef.

Wednesday, take some ground turkey, the cooked quinoa, Dijon mustard, cornichons, and breadcrumbs, and make turkey burgers. Serve in buns or over mixed greens with avocado, nuts, and Parmesan cheese, dressed simply with olive oil and lemon . . . not so bad. Right?

You can even get to Thursday. Just grill up some lamb chops or chicken or beef and use the leftover pesto as a dipping sauce. Or use the leftover quinoa to make **Spring Onion and Quinoa Omelet** (see p. 90). Grill some veggies marinated in olive oil and apple cider vinegar with brown sugar and fresh basil and you are ready to go. Bam!

I have written several cookbooks and done hundreds of cooking shows, and it all comes down to the same thing in the end—a well-stocked kitchen makes cooking dinner on a Tuesday night a breeze, and maybe, just maybe, a little fun. Whether you are gluten-free or not, the key to your success is a good foundation that gives you the tools and confidence to cook great-tasting, nontoxic food.

A few more tips . . .

There are a few more things I want to recommend, mainly ingredients that will make your life easier and your journey into gluten-free eating not soul destroying. Here are some suggestions to help you along the path.

* Keep shredded chicken breasts on hand—I give you two versions, poached and baked (see p. 43).

* Roast your own tomatoes (see p. 79).

* Make homemade gluten-free breadcrumbs—toast gluten-free bread and grind in a food processor with dried herbs.

* Bake off a whack of butternut squash or pumpkin with olive oil and brown sugar to use in soups, pastas, and salads.

* Purée fresh ginger and garlic, add a little olive oil, and store for easy use.

* Precut veggies—peppers, zucchini, onions, mushrooms, for pasta sauces and stir-fries, and store together in Ziploc bags for meal planning and quicker cooking time.

* Roast your own peppers (see p. 30).

* Precook potatoes and sweet potatoes to use in soups, salads, and sauces.

* Make your own reductions—reduce balsamic vinegar, pomegranate juice, and orange juice over heat by about 75 percent for a real burst of flavor.

* Make a big batch of green tea—any kind you like, and keep a pitcher in the refrigerator with fresh lemons and limes for hydration.

Let's see if you've been paying attention

I hope you're starting to get the whole preplanning pantry thing and understand that the kiss of death to being gluten-free is buying premade stuff loaded with crap and, you guessed it, gluten. It's tricky business out there. Some products say they are gluten-free but they have had contact with wheat, which we are trying to stay away from. The best way to avoid mistakes is to know exactly what is in our food.

Enough socializing! Let's get started becoming BFF's with our pantry as we head into our sauce section and lay the groundwork for our gluten-free journey.

AWESOME SAUCES

I am putting this section first because as you progress on your journey into gluten-free healthy eating, you will find it all comes down to flavor. You will begin to taste things differently as your whole approach to food is quietly changing. If you have an arsenal of great sauces, salad dressings, and dips within reach, you are almost halfway there. We will also be using these sauces, dressings, and dips in other recipes. You will find yourself whipping up great meal builders on the spot, effortlessly cooking dinner, managing your new-found health, and generally looking and feeling McAwesome! Sound good? By the way—I made up McAwesome . . . thank you.

RECIPES

DIJON MUSTARD LEMON SWIRL

This is the easiest salad dressing ever, with fans far and wide. You will crave it and, with four ingredients, it will become your go-to favorite. My daughter Lola asks for it at least a few times a week and I use it in my **Magical Mustard Salad** (see p. 164). I also use it as a dressing for cooked green beans and broccoli.

3 Tbsp (45 mL) Dijon mustard
¼ cup (60 mL) extra virgin
   olive oil

½ lemon, juiced
1 tsp (5 mL) balsamic vinegar
Salt to taste

1. Whisk together the mustard, olive oil, lemon juice, and balsamic vinegar until the olive oil is completely blended into the mustard and the dressing becomes a thick paste.

MAKES APPROX. ⅓ CUP (80 ML), ENOUGH FOR 1 PACKAGE OF ARUGULA/SPINACH/MIXED GREEN SALAD

NOTE: Many brands of mustard, including Grey Poupon and French's, are gluten-free.

Why not try...
tossing 2 cups (500 mL) cooked green beans in the mustard dressing, adding ½ cup (125 mL) chopped avocados and ¼ cup (60 mL) toasted almonds. Serve at room temperature.

CLASSIC VINAIGRETTE

VARIATIONS

❦ ❧

SUNDRIED TOMATO DRESSING

Add 2 Tbsp (30 mL) each chopped sundried tomatoes and basil instead of parsley.

MARTINI STRAIGHT UP DRESSING

Add 2 Tbsp (30 mL) chopped olives and ½ tsp (2.5 mL) thyme.

GREEK ISLES

Add 1 Tbsp (15 mL) chopped fresh oregano instead of the parsley, and 2 Tbsp (30 mL) crumbled feta cheese.

MEDITERRANEAN DRESSING

Add 2 Tbsp (30 mL) each chopped roasted red pepper and chopped fresh basil instead of the parsley.

BURST OF LIME

Add 2 Tbsp (30 mL) lime juice instead of the lemon juice, and replace the parsley with fresh cilantro. Also add 1 tsp (5 mL) honey.

Be creative and you will never have to buy salad dressing again.

This is a recipe for a good basic vinaigrette that you can dress up as you like. The fresh herbs, especially the parsley, give it a light, fresh taste. Invest in some Mason jars—they're great for both making and storing your brilliant new salad dressings.

¼ cup (60 mL) red wine vinegar or apple cider vinegar
2 Tbsp (30 mL) lemon juice
1½ Tbsp (22.5 mL) Dijon mustard
2 Tbsp (30 mL) chopped Italian parsley

2 cloves garlic, finely chopped
1 Tbsp (15 mL) minced shallots
1 tsp (5 mL) salt
1 tsp (5 mL) cracked black pepper
1 cup (250 mL) extra virgin olive oil

1. In a small bowl, whisk together all the ingredients except the olive oil. Add the oil slowly, whisking continuously as the dressing thickens.

MAKES APPROX. 1½ CUPS (375 ML)

HAIL CAESAR!

This is a simple low-fat Caesar salad dressing that is made with Greek yogurt. It is light, fresh, and delicious. Use it on romaine lettuce, as a dip for cut up veggies, or as a topping for baked potatoes.

½ cup (125 mL) good quality Parmesan cheese, grated
¼ cup (60 mL) fresh lemon juice
1½ tsp (7.5 mL) grainy mustard
1 small clove garlic
2 anchovy fillets
½ tsp (2.5 mL) sugar

2 Tbsp (30 mL) extra virgin olive oil
½ cup (125 mL) extra thick Greek yogurt
A little salt to taste
Lots of cracked black pepper

1. This recipe can be made in a food processor or using a NutriBullet or hand blender.

2. Mix Parmesan cheese, lemon juice, mustard, garlic, anchovy fillets, and sugar in the food processor until blended.

3. Then add the olive oil and yogurt and blend until all the ingredients are creamy. You can also whisk in the oil and yogurt by hand. Try the dressing and add salt to taste. Finish with lots of cracked black pepper. I use around 1 tsp (5 mL), but adjust to your preference.

MAKES ¾ TO 1 CUP (185 TO 250 ML)

Why not try...making a chicken Caesar salad? Slice up some cooked chicken breast and throw it over romaine lettuce. You can buy gluten-free croutons or make them yourself.

Gluten-Free Croutons

Cut gluten-free bread into 1-inch (2.5 cm) cubes. Toss in a bowl with a little olive oil, salt and pepper, and dried Italian herbs. A nice twist is to use olive oil and a bit of lemon juice for a fresher, lighter taste, with dried oregano or fresh chives. Bake at 375°F (190°C) until crisp and golden, usually 15 to 20 minutes.

CITRUS MASH

This is a light, fresh dressing that's great for summer evenings. I use it in chopped salads and over greens made with denser vegetables like beets or butternut squash when I want to lighten things up. The honey and hint of basil give it a nice bite without being too sweet or heavy. This recipe will dress two or three salads—so you'll always have some in the refrigerator. As I write this, I am inspired by my lemon and orange trees, which will provide the juice for this baby.

1 small shallot, finely chopped
¼ cup (60 mL) rice wine vinegar or apple cider vinegar
5 Tbsp (75 mL) juice of a fresh orange
2 Tbsp (30 mL) lemon juice
2 Tbsp (30 mL) lime juice
1 Tbsp (15 mL) juice of a fresh grapefruit

¾ cup (185 mL) extra virgin olive oil
1 tsp (5 mL) honey
2 tsp (10 mL) chopped fresh basil
½ tsp (2.5 mL) orange or lemon zest
Salt and pepper to taste

1. In a small bowl, whisk together shallot, rice wine vinegar (you can also use apple cider vinegar or white vinegar), orange, lemon, lime, and grapefruit juices. Then add the olive oil slowly as it emulsifies and thickens the dressing. Finish with the honey, chopped basil, and zest. Season with salt and pepper. Store leftover dressing in the refrigerator.

MAKES APPROX. 1 CUP (250 ML)

Why not try...making a quick, easy, light dinner? Take a bag of arugula, some leftover sliced, grilled chicken, black beans, and some crumbled feta cheese and toss in the **Citrus Mash**—delicious!

For an added kick, add some chili flakes.

CANADIAN BACON DRESSING

Why not try...a classic spinach salad? Take a bag of spinach, sliced mushrooms (around 1 cup/250 mL), a couple of hard-boiled eggs, and sliced red onions, and mix together with the warm bacon dressing.

Another great salad is arugula or spinach with fresh figs, pecans, some cherry tomatoes, and grated Parmesan cheese.

All I can say is, thank God bacon is gluten-free. My dad eats it every morning for breakfast and his special bacon skillet is sacred ground. He is also 79 and rail thin. I know there are those out there who do not condone my passion for bacon, and I'm sorry, but I do love it on occasion. You can also get low-fat turkey bacon, naturally smoked organic bacon, maple-infused bacon—the list goes on. For adding flavor and a little fat, bacon is a good standby to have.

4 strips of bacon, diced
1 shallot, diced
¼ cup (60 mL) red wine vinegar
　　or apple cider vinegar
2 Tbsp (30 mL) grainy mustard

1 Tbsp (15 mL) Dijon mustard
1 Tbsp (15 mL) honey
½ tsp (2.5 mL) lemon juice
Salt and pepper to taste

1. In a sauté pan, cook the bacon until crispy. Remove from pan and place on a paper towel to drain.

2. In the bacon fat, cook the shallot until soft, around 3 or 4 minutes.

3. Take the pan off the heat and deglaze it with the vinegar. With a whisk, stir in the grainy mustard, Dijon, honey, and lemon juice until sauce starts to thicken. Add the bacon pieces, season with salt and pepper and serve immediately.

MAKES APPROX. ¾ CUP (185 ML)

ITALIAN HOLIDAY TOMATO SAUCE

This is just a good, classic recipe for a basic tomato sauce that you can elaborate on and make your own. Always buy the best canned tomatoes—it's worth the extra money. Organic and not genetically modified is good. The Italian brands are fantastic—shop around until you find what you like.

¼ cup (60 mL) extra virgin olive oil

1½ cups (375 mL) finely diced onion (about 1 medium onion)

2 cloves garlic

Salt and pepper to taste + extra salt for seasoning

3 Tbsp (45 mL) tomato paste

2 cups (500 mL) fresh basil, chopped

¼ cup (60 mL) red wine

Two 28 oz (794 mL) cans plum tomatoes, chopped, with the liquid

1 tsp (5 mL) dried oregano

2 bay leaves

1 Tbsp (15 mL) balsamic vinegar

1 Tbsp (15 mL) sugar

Amp it up!

In a pan, sauté some bacon and shallots, deglaze with a shot of vodka and add about 2 cups (500 mL) of the sauce.

Bring to a boil, reduce to a simmer and add about ½ cup (125 mL) half-and-half cream. Serve over rigatoni pasta with fresh rosemary and lots of Parmesan cheese and cracked black pepper.

1. Heat oil in a heavy-bottom 4-quart (4 L) pot and cook the onions and garlic together until the onions become translucent, around 5 to 7 minutes. Salt and pepper to taste.

2. Stir in the tomato paste and coat the onion mixture well.

3. Add the fresh basil and sauté for 1 to 2 minutes.

4. Deglaze the pan with the red wine.

5. Add the tomatoes, oregano, bay leaves, balsamic vinegar, and sugar, and bring the sauce to a boil.

6. Reduce the heat to a simmer and cook for about 1 hour, checking every 8 minutes or so to make sure it's not burning. Season with salt and remove the bay leaves.

MAKES APPROX. 3½ CUPS (875 ML)

NOTE: This sauce is fresh and delicious and a great base to experiment with to make other sauces.

BASIL CASHEW PESTO

Why not try...making a quick and easy dip? Take 2 to 3 Tbsp (30 to 45 mL) of the pesto and mix it into cream cheese or thick Greek yogurt. Add some finely chopped red pepper for freshness and color. Serve with veggies or warm corn chips.

One of my favorite things, especially in the summer, is pesto. It is super easy to make and is great on pasta, salads, vegetables, and chicken and fish. I make arugula pesto, avocado pesto, roasted red pepper pesto, and I am even including a mushroom pesto, because I am crazy about fungi. This recipe makes a good basic pesto but taste as you go—some people prefer a drier pesto, while others like it more fluid, using more olive oil, or more garlic and less basil. Figure out what you like and modify it as you become more familiar with the process. FYI—my friends beg me to make this whenever I invite them over for cocktails and dinner.

4 cups (1 L) fresh basil
1 cup (250 mL) arugula
1 clove garlic
1 lemon, juiced
½ cup (125 mL) toasted cashew
    nuts (see p. 24)

¼ cup (60 mL) toasted pine
    nuts (see p. 24)
½ to ¾ cup (125 to 185 mL)
    extra virgin olive oil
¾ cup (185 mL) grated
    Parmesan cheese
Salt and pepper to taste

1. Preheat the oven to 350°F (175°C).

2. In a food processor, combine the basil, arugula, garlic, lemon juice, toasted nuts, olive oil, and Parmesan cheese. Blend thoroughly, season to taste with salt and pepper, and serve fresh.

MAKES APPROX. 2½ CUPS (625 ML)

NOTE: If you have leftovers, place in an airtight container with 1 Tbsp (15 mL) olive oil to keep it fresh and store in the refrigerator.

ROSEMARY BALSAMIC HUMMUS

This delicious recipe is courtesy of my lovely friend Denise. She and her "forever husband" (her words) Lee own a food shop called The Market, in Lakefield, Ontario, a town near our family's country house. It is the most beautiful store ever and they may be the cutest couple I know—my daughter Lola is crazy about them. This hummus is unique and flavorful and very low in fat—no tahini involved. I guess this is how Denise keeps her smokin' shape and, come to think of it, her husband Lee . . .

2 sprigs fresh rosemary
1 clove garlic
Two 15 oz (425 mL) cans
  chickpeas

¼ cup (60 mL) extra virgin
  olive oil
¼ cup (60 mL) balsamic vinegar
¼ cup (60 mL) water
Salt and black pepper to taste

1. Purée all ingredients in a food processor. It's pretty served with a drizzle of balsamic glaze and a little sprig of fresh rosemary.

MAKES APPROX. 3 CUPS (750 ML)

BALSAMIC MUSHROOM PESTO

Why not try . . . serving over angel hair pasta with lots of cracked black pepper and roasted cherry tomatoes? Top with some toasted pine nuts and prepare to be in heaven.

This is a different take on pesto. For years I was making roasted red pepper pesto and then I decided to give mushrooms a shot. The result is a smoky rich pesto that's great on pasta, or served with chicken or grilled organic beef. I also use a dollop as a garnish for soup, or to top a baked potato. It is my most requested pesto. Who knew?

4 cups (1 L) mushrooms, chopped (use a mix of button, shitake, and portobello)
3 Tbsp (45 mL) butter
3 Tbsp (45 mL) balsamic vinegar
1½ cups (375 mL) fresh basil
1 cup (250 mL) arugula
2 cloves garlic
1 Tbsp (15 mL) lemon juice

1 Tbsp (15 mL) honey
½ to ¾ cup (125 to 185 mL) extra virgin olive oil
½ cup (125 mL) toasted almonds, pine nuts or cashews (see p. 24)
½ cup (125 mL) grated Parmesan cheese
Salt and pepper to taste

1.   In a medium-sized pan over medium heat, sauté the chopped mushrooms in the butter until they start to soften, approx. 3 to 5 minutes. Season with salt and pepper.

2.   Deglaze the pan with the balsamic vinegar and continue cooking until the mushrooms absorb the liquid, another 3 to 5 minutes. Let cool for 5 minutes.

3.   In a food processor, add the basil, arugula, garlic, lemon juice, honey, olive oil, toasted nuts, Parmesan cheese, and the sautéed mushrooms. Blend thoroughly, season to taste with salt and pepper, and serve fresh.

MAKES 2 CUPS (500 ML)

Toasting Nuts and Seeds

Certain recipes throughout the book call for toasted nuts and seeds in their ingredients. Here's a quick primer on how to correctly toast a variety of nuts and seeds:

Almonds—Heat your oven to 350°F (175°C) and place almonds on a baking sheet. Bake for 12 to 15 minutes, shaking every 5 minutes until almonds turn golden.

Cashews—Heat your oven to 350°F (175°C) and place cashews on a baking sheet. Bake for 12 to 15 minutes, shaking every 5 minutes until cashews turn golden.

Walnuts—Heat your oven to 350°F (175°C) and place walnuts on a baking sheet. Bake for 8 to 10 minutes, but check the nuts at 5 minutes and shake around. Check again 2 to 3 minutes later.

Pecans—Heat your oven to 350°F (175°C) and place pecans on a baking sheet. Bake for 5 to 8 minutes, checking at 3 to 4 minutes as pecans toast quickly and you do not want to scorch.

Pine Nuts—These can be tricky and can burn quickly. Heat your oven to 350°F (175°C) and place pine nuts on a baking sheet. Bake for 5 to 7 minutes, but check every 2 to 3 minutes so as not to burn! Keep an eye on these babies!

Sesame Seeds—Toast seeds in a dry skillet over medium heat for 3 to 5 minutes until lightly browned, stirring occasionally. Alternatively, you can bake the seeds on an ungreased baking sheet at 350°F (175°C) for 8 to 10 minutes or until lightly browned. Watch to avoid scorching.

HOISIN FOR DAYS

If you're going to cook gluten-free, you have to have some basic sauces handy, and hoisin is one of them—for all your Asian stir-fries, marinades, and noodle dishes. You also need to get acquainted with Chinese five-spice powder. It is so authentic, and a flavor enhancer for all your culinary experiments. Hoisin sauce is really simple to make and completely healthy. Make up a batch for the week and use when needed. It is soooo delicious! You will become addicted . . . I promise.

5 Tbsp (75 mL) gluten-free tamari sauce

2 Tbsp (30 mL) organic peanut butter (I also use almond butter)

1 Tbsp (15 mL) honey or molasses

2 Tbsp (30 mL) maple syrup

2 tsp (10 mL) rice wine vinegar or apple cider vinegar

2 tsp (10 mL) sesame oil

½ tsp (2.5 mL) Chinese five-spice powder

1 clove garlic, minced

1 Tbsp (15 mL) canola oil

Gluten-free hot sauce to taste

Cracked black pepper to taste

1. In a small bowl, mix together the tamari, peanut butter, honey (or molasses), maple syrup, rice wine vinegar (or apple cider vinegar), and sesame oil.

2. In a small pan, sauté the five-spice powder and garlic in the canola oil until the aroma from the spices is released, about 1 minute.

3. Add the mixture from the bowl to the pan and slowly stir with a whisk at a medium-low heat for about 3 to 4 minutes, until the sauce begins to thicken and brown. Mix together well. Add hot sauce and black pepper to taste.

MAKES APPROX. ½ CUP (125 ML)

PEANUT ENVY

God, I love this sauce! It is essential for gluten-free cooking to have a good peanut sauce in your arsenal. Whether you use it for stir-fries, noodle dishes, or marinades, this sauce is loved by all ages. Make up a whole batch for the week and store it in your refrigerator until needed. Mason jars! Get some.

1 cup (250 mL) natural peanut
   butter
½ tsp (2.5 mL) gluten-free hot
   sauce or chili flakes to taste
¼ cup (60 mL) gluten-free
   tamari sauce

½ cup (125 mL) coconut milk
2 limes, juiced
1 Tbsp (15 mL) honey
1 clove garlic
½ tsp (2.5 mL) sesame oil
½ cup (125 mL) fresh cilantro

Why not try...spicing up Tuesday's dinner? Julienne about 2 to 3 cups (500 to 750 mL) cucumbers, carrots, and red peppers. Quarter 2 hard-boiled eggs. Toss veggies in peanut sauce; serve in the middle of a platter surrounded by the eggs. Garnish with salty peanuts and fresh cilantro.

1.   Combine the peanut butter, hot sauce (or chili flakes), tamari sauce, coconut milk, lime juice, honey, garlic, sesame oil, and cilantro in a food processor. Blend until smooth.

MAKES 2 CUPS (500 ML)

ASIAN ORANGE SAUCE

Now that you're cooking and eating healthier, you'll probably get addicted to stir-fries. They're easy and economical and a great way to use your cooking creativity. I have added some black beans to the sauce to give it an extra boost of protein. This sauce is citrus heaven.

2 Tbsp (30 mL) chopped ginger
2 small cloves garlic, finely chopped
¼ cup (60 mL) gluten-free tamari sauce
½ cup (125 mL) **Hoisin For Days** sauce (see p. 25)
½ to ¾ cups (125 to 185 mL) freshly squeezed orange juice (I like it really orangey, so I use ¾ cup)

1 lime, juiced
¾ cup (185 mL) black beans, cooked (instructions follow)
2 Tbsp (30 mL) honey or maple syrup
1 Tbsp (15 mL) gluten-free flour (optional)

1. In a food processor, combine ginger, garlic, tamari sauce, hoisin sauce, orange juice, lime juice, black beans, and honey. Blend until smooth.

2. Transfer to a saucepan and bring to a boil, then simmer for approx. 5 minutes. If you want a thicker sauce add 1 Tbsp (15 mL) gluten-free flour. Mix with a little warm water first to dilute the flour so it doesn't make the sauce lumpy. Add slowly to desired thickness.

MAKES 1½ TO 2 CUPS (375 TO 500 ML)

Cooking Beans and Lentils

Certain recipes call for cooked beans and lentils of different varieties. The following are suggested procedures for prepping your beans properly:

Lentils (brown)—1 cup (250 mL) dry lentils to 3 cups (750 mL) water. No soaking necessary. To cook, simmer for 30 minutes. Yields 2 to 2½ cups (500 to 625 mL) cooked lentils.

Lentils (red)—1 cup (250 mL) dry lentils to 2 cups (500 mL) salted water. No soaking required as lentils are already hulled and split. Bring to a boil and cook for 20 to 25 minutes until they start to get mushy. Yields 2½ to 3 cups (625 to 750 mL) cooked lentils.

Black Beans—1 cup (250 mL) dry beans to 4 cups (1 L) water. Soak overnight and drain. Cook in fresh water, simmering for 60 to 90 minutes. Yields 2½ to 3 cups (625 mL to 750 mL) cooked beans.

Garbanzo Beans (chickpeas)—1 cup (250 mL) dry beans to 4 cups (1 L) water. Soak overnight and drain. Cook in fresh water, simmering for 2 to 3 hours. Yields 3 cups (750 mL) cooked beans.

Kidney Beans—1 cup (250 mL) dry beans to 3 cups (750 mL) water. You can soak overnight or skip the soak and cook straight away. Soaked, cooking time is 60+ minutes. Unsoaked, cooking time is 90 minutes. Yields 2½ cups (625 mL) cooked beans.

Split Peas—1 cup (250 mL) dry beans to 3 cups (750 mL) water. No soaking required. Cooking time is 45 to 75 minutes. Yields 2½ cups (625 mL) cooked split peas.

ROASTED RED PEPPER SAUCE

Amp it up!

Heat up the sauce and serve it over penne with lots of cracked pepper and wilted arugula.

Another great pasta dish is grilled eggplant and linguine. Top with the roasted red pepper sauce, a few slices of fresh mozzarella, and a sprig of rosemary.

Roasted Red Peppers

To roast peppers, preheat your oven to 500°F (260°C), line a baking sheet with aluminum foil, and roast the peppers for about 12 to 15 minutes until they start to blacken. I usually throw on a little olive oil and kosher salt, but that's up to you. Allow to cool and then rub off the black skins. It's always a good idea to roast a bunch as they are great in salads, sauces, and dips. Store in a Mason jar with a little olive oil.

I got such grief over this sauce from my picky friends who had never dared to try a red pepper sauce—they were purists and if it was red it had to be tomato! But they shut up after they tried it. It has smoky roasted peppers as its base, with some sundried tomatoes thrown in. This is a slightly chunky sauce that is great for pasta, and is also good as a dipping sauce for barbecued chicken or beef.

½ cup (125 mL) chopped green onion
2 roasted red peppers, chopped and seeded (see sidebar)
¼ cup (60 mL) sundried tomatoes in oil
1 cup (250 mL) gluten-free chicken or veggie stock
1 cup (250 mL) coconut milk or half-and-half cream
1 tsp (5 mL) chili flakes (for a kick)
½ cup (125 mL) chopped fresh basil
1 tsp (5 mL) dried oregano
¼ cup (60 mL) toasted pine nuts (see p. 24)
½ cup (125 mL) grated Parmesan cheese
Salt and pepper to taste

1. In a food processor, combine green onion, roasted red peppers, sundried tomatoes, stock, coconut milk, chili flakes, basil, oregano, toasted pine nuts, and Parmesan. Blend until you get a nice chunky, yet consistent sauce. Season with salt and pepper to taste.

MAKES APPROX. 3 CUPS (750 ML)

ST. TROPEZ SIESTA

This is one of my favorite cold sauces and the perfect companion to a scooped-out avocado. Light and refreshing, it can be made ahead of time and used for a myriad of dishes. Grab a Pimm's and a croquet mallet, wear white, and whisper. You will begin to relax immediately.

Two 6 oz (170 g) cans of high quality crab meat (drained really well and patted dry)
½ cup (125 mL) capers
1 lemon, juiced
½ cup (125 mL) mayonnaise
½ cup (125 mL) Greek yogurt or sour cream
½ cup (125 mL) fresh basil
½ cup (125 mL) chives
1 Tbsp (15 mL) extra virgin olive oil
Salt and pepper to taste

1. In a food processor, combine the crab, capers, lemon juice, mayo, yogurt, basil, chives, olive oil, and salt and pepper. Blend until fairly smooth.

2. Refrigerate in an airtight container topped with a little olive oil.

MAKES 1½ TO 2 CUPS (375 TO 500 ML)

Why not try ...August lunch? Cut up 5 ripe vine tomatoes into ½-inch (1 cm) thick slices and arrange on a platter. Put 1 Tbsp (15 mL) of the sauce on each tomato and top with a slice of sundried tomato and a fresh chive.

You could also use this sauce as a base for potato salad. Take 2 cups (500 mL) cooked diced potatoes, ½ cup (125 mL) finely diced red onions, and ¼ cup (60 mL) crumbled cooked bacon. Toss well and garnish with black pepper and some fresh chives. Potato decadence!

LEMON FETA DIP

Amp it up!

Serve in a gluten-free wrap
with lemon rosemary chicken
and grilled eggplant or zucchini.
For the chicken, marinate
skewer-sized pieces in olive
oil, lemon juice, rosemary, and
salt and pepper. Grill them up,
cut them up, and serve them up,
inside the wrap.

This dip is a great staple. It works well on its own or with other dips. Easy to whip up, it is very versatile, delicious in sandwich wraps, with grilled chicken and lamb, or all on its own.

6 oz (170 g) crumbled feta
cheese
¾ cup (185 mL) Greek yogurt
¼ cup (60 mL) shelled
pistachios

½ lemon, juiced
1 tsp (5 mL) lemon zest
1 clove garlic
2 Tbsp (30 mL) fresh dill
Salt and pepper to taste

1. Combine the feta, yogurt, pistachios, lemon juice, lemon zest, garlic, and fresh dill in a food processor. Blend until smooth and creamy. Salt and pepper to taste.

MAKES APPROX. 1½ CUPS (375 ML)

ROASTED GARLIC PASTE

This is a great way to pack a big punch of flavor. I like this because I am not the biggest garlic fan—I think it is really overused. But when you roast garlic, it becomes sweet and smoky and not as harsh. You will become addicted to this cooking staple—make a huge batch and use it to tart up all your new recipes.

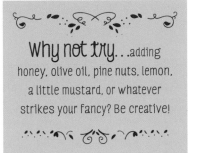

why not try...adding honey, olive oil, pine nuts, lemon, a little mustard, or whatever strikes your fancy? Be creative!

10 to 12 heads of garlic
1 to 2 Tbsp (15 to 30 mL)
    olive oil

Salt and pepper to taste

1. Preheat the oven to 350°F (175°C).

2. Cut off the tops of the garlic heads and drizzle with olive oil. Salt and pepper to taste. Wrap in aluminum foil and bake for about 90 minutes.

3. When cool, squeeze out the garlic and mix well in a food processor.

MAKES APPROX. 1½ CUPS (375 ML)

GETTING IT UP! YOUR COURAGE, THAT IS . . .

TEN CONFIDENCE-BUILDING RECIPES

The important thing now is to jump right in. We are going to take the intimidation factor out of gluten-free cooking, remembering that our goal is to use whole, healthy, unprocessed foods. You can get great basics—gluten-free bread, pasta, flour, and spices—without compromising taste and substance. It will also be a lesson in reading labels—just because it's gluten-free doesn't mean it's good for you, especially if it's loaded with sugars, fructose, and tons of sodium or fat. A lot of people who are gluten-free don't digest soy well, so, whenever possible, I will provide a substitute. Let's get started with something a little unusual but so easy to do . . .

RECIPES

THE BEST FAKE RISOTTO YOU WILL EVER TASTE

This is a great dish when you don't have a lot of time to stand around. I learned this trick in a French restaurant I worked in—we called it risotto, but, um, technically . . . it wasn't. But it was and is delicious and has the same creamy consistency that a good risotto has. I have decided that I am going to give it a little Thai twist to up your game . . . okay?

1½ cups (375 mL) uncooked long grain rice

2 Tbsp (30 mL) sesame oil

½ cup (125 mL) chopped shallots

⅓ cup (80 mL) chopped green onions + extra for garnish

2 Tbsp (30 mL) grated ginger

1 clove garlic, chopped

2 cups (500 mL) cooked, shredded chicken breasts (see p. 44)

1 lime, juiced

¼ cup (60 mL) gluten-free tamari sauce

1¾ cups (435 mL) crushed tomatoes

1 cup (250 mL) coconut milk

Salt and pepper to taste

½ cup (125 mL) chopped fresh cilantro

¼ cup (60 mL) chopped fresh basil

1 cup (250 mL) grated Swiss cheese

Cracked black pepper for garnish

(see p. 44)

1. Cook the rice in 3 cups (750 mL) water according to the instructions on the package and set aside.

2. In a large sauté pan, heat the sesame oil and sauté the shallots and green onions until soft.

3. Add the ginger and the garlic and sauté for another 3 minutes.

4. Add the chicken and cook for another 2 to 3 minutes. Add the lime juice, tamari sauce, tomatoes, and coconut milk, and season with salt and pepper. Bring to a boil.

5. Reduce to medium heat and add the cooked rice, cilantro, basil, and cheese, and continue cooking until you get a nice creamy mixture. Garnish with a sprinkling of chopped green onions and fresh cracked black pepper. Serve warm and lie to your guests!

MAKES 4 TO 6 SERVINGS

More Vitamin C, Please

Serve this with a shredded papaya salad. Shred 2 cups (500 mL) not-too-ripe papaya, slice ½ cup (125 mL) red pepper, ¼ cup (60 mL) red onion, and toss in olive oil, lime juice, and salt and pepper. Garnish with lots of fresh cilantro and salted peanuts. You can also use mango.

WALNUT TACOS WITH AVOCADO FOAM

We're officially stepping out of our comfort zone and trying some delicious, healthy alternatives to what we usually eat. Everywhere I go, I meet people who have a story about health and adjusting their diets. This recipe is from Jack's dentist, a lovely young woman who went through a phase where she could not even get out of bed. Turns out she had Hashimoto's disease, an autoimmune disorder that affects the thyroid. Her hair was falling out, she was beyond fatigued, and she had tons of digestive issues. After going to a naturopath, she went gluten-free—veggies, salads, corn tortillas, fruits, and lots of quinoa! Within nine months she had reversed her disease through eating clean—her doctor was amazed. To this day, if she falls off her regime, the same old problems creep back. This is one of her favorite recipes—and now it's one of mine too.

Why not try…serving the taco filling over greens and diced avocados, with grated raw cheddar cheese and fresh cilantro. Dress with olive oil and lime juice.

2 cups (500 mL) organic walnuts, presoaked (see note)
½ cup (125 mL) sundried tomatoes (see note)
2 Tbsp (30 mL) olive oil, divided
1 to 2 tsp (5 to 10 mL) **Homemade Taco Mix** (recipe follows)
¼ cup (60 mL) fresh cilantro, chopped

8 to 12 gluten-free corn taco shells
1½ to 2 cups (375 to 500 mL) **Avocado Foam** (recipe follows)
Suggested garnish: arugula, chopped tomatoes, grilled corn, shredded lettuce, chopped red onions

1. To make the taco filling, put the presoaked walnuts (make sure to dry them well first), sundried tomatoes, 1 Tbsp (15 mL) olive oil, and the **Homemade Taco Mix** into a food processor and blend into a chunky paste. Taste and season with more taco mix if desired. Add the fresh cilantro and blend again.

2. Heat taco shells in a 350°F (175°C) oven until warm, about 5 to 7 minutes.

Continued on next page ↜

3. In a skillet over a medium-low heat, sauté the taco filling mixture in 1 Tbsp (15 mL) olive oil until warm. Salt and pepper to taste and set aside.

4. Fill the warmed-up taco shells with taco filling. Top with a dollop of the **Avocado Foam** and any of the suggested garnishes.

MAKES 8 TO 12 TACOS

NOTE: Soak the walnuts in water for about 1 to 2 hours to draw out all the toxins. Before use, dry thoroughly.

NOTE: Buy sundried tomatoes in oil or in dried form. If they are dried, soak in water for a couple hours to soften. If you are doing a big batch, store in a Mason jar with olive oil. Add some chilies for a kick!

HOMEMADE TACO MIX

1 Tbsp (15 mL) chili powder
1 tsp (5 mL) paprika
1 tsp (5 mL) ground cumin
½ tsp (2.5 mL) ground coriander
½ tsp (2.5 mL) dried oregano
¼ to ¾ tsp (1 to 4 mL) cayenne
  pepper (adjust for heat)

½ tsp (2.5 mL) garlic powder
  (or fresh—1 small clove garlic,
  finely chopped)
¼ tsp (1 mL) onion powder (or
  2 Tbsp/30 mL finely chopped
  fresh onion)
1 tsp (5 mL) sea salt
1 tsp (5 mL) ground black
  pepper

1. Blend all the taco mix ingredients together. Personalize by adjusting the heat and ratio of ingredients. Use immediately or store in an airtight container.

MAKES APPROX. 3 TBSP (45 ML)

AVOCADO FOAM

2 ripe avocados
1 cup (250 mL) Greek yogurt
1 Tbsp (15 mL) finely chopped
　　fresh cilantro

1 tsp (5 mL) smoked paprika
1 to 2 tsp (5 to 10 mL) fresh
　　lime juice

1. Blend the avocado (without the pit!), yogurt, and chopped cilantro in a blender or NutriBullet until smooth. Place in a dish, squeeze on some fresh lime juice and dust with the paprika. Set aside.

MAKES 2½ TO 3 CUPS (625 TO 750 ML)

THAI NOODLE SALAD

This is Jack and Lola's favorite recipe and one of the easiest things to make if you are having a crowd of people over at the last minute. It also introduces another one of my staples—shredded chicken. It will begin to save your life with all the meals it can transform and tart up. The dressing is my classic **Peanut Envy** sauce.

14 oz (394 g) dried gluten-free spaghetti
1 tsp (5 mL) sesame oil
2 chicken breasts, shredded (recipes for **Poached** and **Baked Shredded Chicken** follow)
1 cup (250 mL) julienned carrots
1 red pepper, julienned

½ an English cucumber, julienned
¾ cup (185 mL) fresh cilantro, chopped + extra for garnish (optional)
¾ to 1 cup (185 to 250 mL) **Peanut Envy** sauce (see p. 27)
½ cup (125 mL) bean sprouts
¼ cup (60 mL) salted or roasted peanuts, chopped
Cracked black pepper to taste

1. Cook pasta in a large pot of boiling, salted water until al dente, approx. 8 to 10 minutes. Drain, run under cold water, allow to dry, and sprinkle with the sesame oil.

2. Place the cooked noodles in a large bowl. Layer the shredded chicken on top with the carrots, pepper, cucumbers, and cilantro. Toss well with the **Peanut Envy** sauce.

3. Transfer to a colorful platter and garnish with the bean sprouts, peanuts, and cracked black pepper. Add extra cilantro if you like. You will be so impressed with yourself.

MAKES 4 TO 6 SERVINGS

Continued on next page ✎

POACHED SHREDDED CHICKEN

Poaching, rather than baking (see next page), gives you a lighter version of shredded chicken because you use stock instead of olive oil. I use both methods and it's personal preference as to which one works better for you. I find that baking, however, gives it more flavor.

Gluten-free chicken or veggie stock (enough to cover the chicken)
1 small onion, roughly chopped

2 skinless, boneless chicken breasts
½ lime, juiced
Salt and pepper to taste

1. In a pan, bring the stock and the roughly chopped onion to a boil. Add the chicken and lime juice and simmer on medium-low with the lid on until the chicken is done, approx. 25 to 35 minutes depending on thickness. Turn the chicken over halfway through cooking.

2. When the chicken has cooled, take two forks and shred the hell out of it! Sprinkle with a little salt and pepper.

MAKES 2½ TO 3 CUPS (625 TO 750 ML)

BAKED SHREDDED CHICKEN OR CUBED CHICKEN

2 skinless, boneless chicken
  breasts
½ lemon, juiced
2 Tbsp (30 mL) olive oil

1 tsp (5 mL) chopped
  fresh thyme
Salt and pepper to taste

1. Preheat the oven to 385°F (195°C).

2. In a bowl, mix together chicken, lemon juice, olive oil, thyme, and salt and pepper.

3. Place on a baking dish and bake in the oven for 40 to 50 minutes until done. Allow to cool and then shred with a fork, or you can cut the chicken into ½- to 1-inch (1 to 2.5 cm) cubes, depending on preference.

MAKES 2½ TO 3 CUPS (625 TO 750 ML)

MUSHROOM ARUGULA FRITTATA

Why not try...roasted red peppers and eggplant with basil and goat cheese? Or pancetta and onions and Swiss cheese? Be creative!

I love frittatas! There, I've said it. They are the easiest thing ever and come in lots of configurations. They can be perfect for a light dinner or a more substantial meal, depending on your ingredients. They are excellent brunch fare and actually allow you to spend time with your guests instead of being chained to your stove. It's egg feminism!

6 eggs
1 Tbsp (15 mL) olive oil
2 Tbsp (30 mL) chopped fresh basil
Salt and cracked black pepper to taste, divided
½ cup (125 mL) finely chopped onions
3 Tbsp (45 mL) olive oil

3 cups (750 mL) mushrooms, chopped
1 tsp (5 mL) dried oregano
2 cups (500 mL) arugula
½ cup (125 mL) goat cheese
½ cup (125 mL) grated Parmesan cheese
¼ cup (60 mL) toasted pine nuts for garnish (see p. 24)

1. In a bowl, whisk together the eggs, olive oil, fresh basil, and salt and pepper to taste, then get ready to go!

2. In a large non-stick pan over medium heat, sauté the onions in the olive oil until they begin to soften.

3. Add the mushrooms, dried oregano, and salt and pepper, and sauté until the mushrooms are mostly cooked, around 3 to 5 minutes.

4. Add the arugula to the mushroom mixture. Sauté until the arugula wilts, about 3 minutes.

5. Pour the egg mixture into the pan, stirring to lightly scramble the eggs. As the eggs start to cook, add the goat cheese. Pull the egg mixture away from the edges of the pan into the center so the uncooked eggs can spill over and cook. Do this until the eggs are evenly cooked and fairly firm and begin to pull away from the sides—about 4 to 6 minutes.

6. Sprinkle with the grated Parmesan cheese and broil in the oven for about 2 to 3 minutes, until the frittata rises, is firm, and the cheese is golden on top.

7. Garnish with cracked black pepper and toasted pine nuts.

MAKES 4 SERVINGS

ROASTED CURRIED CAULIFLOWER SOUP

This is one of my favorite soups ever. It is easy and so delicious, with the roasted flavor of the cauliflower and the sweetness of the curry. I have been known to go on a soup binge and eat it for days. It is very hearty, so get ready to be cozy.

2 heads of cauliflower, chopped

3 Tbsp (45 mL) olive oil, divided

2 tsp (10 mL) kosher or sea salt + extra for seasoning

1 onion, chopped

2 Tbsp (30 mL) gluten-free curry paste (or use the **Curry Paste** recipe that follows)

2 Tbsp (30 mL) brown sugar or maple syrup

7 to 8 cups (1.75 to 2 L) gluten-free chicken or veggie stock

Crostini for garnish (recipe follows)

1. Preheat the oven to 400°F (200°C). On a baking sheet lined with aluminum foil, spread the chopped cauliflower evenly. Drizzle with 2 Tbsp (30 mL) olive oil and 2 tsp (10 mL) salt. Bake for approx. 25 to 30 minutes, until the cauliflower starts to turn golden.

2. In a large soup pot, sauté the onion in the remaining 1 Tbsp (15 mL) olive oil until it begins to soften. Season with salt and a little pepper.

3. Add the curry paste, sugar (or maple syrup), and coat the onions well (see note at end of recipe).

4. Add the roasted cauliflower and coat well with the onion and curry mixture. Add the stock and bring to a vigorous boil.

5. Lower to a medium simmer and reduce the soup by approx. one-third, until it has a thick and creamy consistency, usually 25 to 30 minutes. Check frequently so it does not reduce too much.

6. While the soup simmers, prepare **Crostini** (recipe follows).

7. When the soup is reduced, remove from heat, wait until it cools, then purée with a blender to a creamy consistency.

8. Serve the soup in bowls with **Crostini** on top as a garnish.

MAKES 4 SERVINGS

NOTE: When making your own curry paste for recipes, you might have to adjust the sweetness of the dish. For example in the **Roasted Curried Cauliflower Soup**, you might only need 1 Tbsp (15 mL) sugar instead of 2, or you might want more—let your own taste determine the amount.

NOTE: When making soups, it is always better if the consistency is too thick after puréeing—you can always add more liquid/stock/cream later to get the desired thickness.

CURRY PASTE

1 Tbsp (15 mL) curry powder
1 tsp (5 mL) olive oil

2 tsp (10 mL) brown sugar
½ lime, juiced

1. Mix the curry powder, olive oil, brown sugar, and lime juice into a paste.

MAKES 2 TBSP (30 ML)

CROSTINI

2 slices gluten-free bread
1 to 2 Tbsp (15 to 30 mL)
  olive oil
Salt to taste

1 Tbsp (15 mL) chopped fresh
  rosemary
⅓ cup (80 mL) goat cheese
  (optional)

1. Cut the gluten-free bread into 4 even pieces, 8 crostini in total. Brush with olive oil, a little salt, and chopped rosemary. Bake in a 400°F (200°C) oven until golden, about 5 to 7 minutes. Serve with a sprinkle of goat cheese on top, if desired.

MAKES 8 CROSTINI

CHICKEN À LA GARRETT SWANN

FROM THE SANTA BARBARA SWANNS—TWO N'S, DARLING!

Why not try...serving this with basil roasted potatoes? Cube about 3 cups (750 mL) of Yukon Gold potatoes (cut into 1-inch/2.5 cm cubes). Toss in olive oil and 1 to 2 tsp (5 to 10 mL) dried basil, and salt and pepper. Bake for about 50 to 60 minutes (shaking the pan every 20 minutes or so) at 400°F (200°C) until crispy and golden. You can also use dried oregano or fresh basil!

This fabulous chicken piccata recipe is courtesy of my bestie Garrett Swann. He cooked my family dinner one night and made it gluten-free for his partner in crime, Miss Lola. She loved it but loved it even more when he played *Angry Birds* with her for two hours—but guess who cleaned up?

2 eggs
1½ cups (375 mL) gluten-free flour
1 tsp (5 mL) dried Italian herb seasoning
Salt and pepper to taste
4 pieces thinly pounded skinless, boneless chicken breasts

6 to 8 Tbsp (90 to 120 mL) unsalted butter, divided (approx. 1 stick)
3 Tbsp (45 mL) olive oil
½ cup (125 mL) capers
2 lemons, juiced (I like it really lemony)

1. Preheat the oven to 375°F (190°C).

2. Whisk the eggs together in a bowl and pour into a shallow baking dish.

3. In another shallow baking dish, mix together the flour, herb seasoning, and salt and pepper.

4. Coat the chicken with the egg mixture and then dredge in the flour and coat evenly.

5. In a large sauté pan over medium heat, combine olive oil with 2 to 3 Tbsp (30 to 45 mL) butter. Put in 4 pieces of chicken breast and cook 3 to 4 minutes per side until golden brown and cooked.

6. When done, keep the cooked chicken warm in the oven until your sauce is prepared.

7. In the pan where you have cooked the chicken, put in the remaining butter, approx. 4 to 5 Tbsp (60 to 75 mL), and sauté the capers on medium-low heat—you do not want the sauce to separate. Add the lemon juice slowly and cook 2 to 3 minutes longer so the sauce thickens with the butter and the drippings from the chicken.

8. Remove chicken from the oven and plate, pouring the sauce over it. Yummy!

MAKES 4 SERVINGS

NOTE: You can get the chicken pounded by your butcher, or buy it already done, or do it yourself—the thinner and more evenly pounded it is, the better it is for texture and even cooking.

TURKEY SKEWERS WITH COCONUT BEAN MASH

Why not try...serving with gluten-free wraps or corn tortillas or gluten-free pitas? Persian cucumbers are delicious as a side to this dish!

Tzatziki

For a quick tzatziki dipping sauce combine 1 cup (250 mL) yogurt, 1 minced garlic clove, ½ cup (125 mL) shredded cucumber, 1 Tbsp (15 mL) olive oil, 1 Tbsp (15 mL) lemon juice, some chopped fresh dill, and salt and pepper to taste.

I love these skewers—they remind me of being somewhere exotic and not being hunted down by my children for pick-up and Starbucks. I am daydreaming right now about being on the isle of Mykonos, eating lunch overlooking the Mediterranean while my hot Greek boyfriend grills my skewers . . .

12 wooden skewers
10 oz (300 g) ground turkey
1 onion, finely chopped
1 Tbsp (15 mL) chopped fresh cilantro
2 Tbsp (30 mL) chopped fresh parsley

½ tsp (2.5 mL) ground cumin
1 Tbsp (15 mL) Dijon mustard
1 tsp (5 mL) prepared horseradish
Salt and pepper to taste
1 to 2 Tbsp (15 to 30 mL) olive oil

1. Before you begin, soak about 12 wooden skewers for 45 minutes to an hour so they won't burn.

2. In a food processor, put the turkey, onion, cilantro, parsley, ground cumin, mustard, horseradish, and salt and pepper. Process until fully blended.

3. Divide the mixture into 12 portions. Wet your hands a little and shape each portion around a skewer.

4. Cover and chill for an hour.

5. Heat up a grill pan or your barbecue to a medium heat and brush with the olive oil. Grill the skewers for about 10 to 12 minutes, turning occasionally until they are nicely browned and cooked through. Serve with **Cannellini Coconut Mash Up** (recipe follows).

MAKES 12 TURKEY SKEWERS

Continued on next page ↝

CANNELLINI COCONUT MASH UP

1 Tbsp (15 mL) olive oil
1 clove garlic
One 15 oz (425 mL) can
    cannellini beans, rinsed and
    drained
½ cup (125 mL) canned
    chickpeas

¼ cup (60 mL) coconut milk
¼ tsp (1 mL) chili flakes
    (optional)
2 Tbsp (30 mL) chopped fresh
    cilantro
Salt and pepper to taste

1. In a large saucepan, heat up the olive oil and sauté the garlic.

2. Add the cannellini beans, chickpeas, and coconut milk and heat for a few minutes. For a kick you can add some chili flakes if you like.

3. Transfer to a food processor and blend with the fresh cilantro until smooth. Salt and pepper to taste.

MAKES APPROX. 1½ CUPS (375 ML)

PARISIAN DELIGHT PIZZA

This pizza is so simple, so addictive, and so perfect for parties and last minute soirées that you will never serve anything else. Just get some gluten-free pizza crust and use your imagination!

½ cup (125 mL) gluten-free
  Dijon mustard
1 frozen gluten-free pizza crust
1½ cups (375 mL) thinly-sliced
  Black Forest ham
2 cups (500 mL) raw Swiss
  cheese, shredded (or use
  regular Swiss cheese,
  depending on your tolerance)

½ cup (125 mL) thinly-sliced
  red onion
Freshly ground black pepper
  to taste
Fresh thyme or basil for garnish

1. Preheat the oven to 375°F (190°C).

2. Spread the mustard evenly over the pizza crust. Top with Black Forest ham strips, Swiss cheese, and red onion. Sprinkle with black pepper. Place in the oven on a baking sheet, or on the rack if you want a crispier crust.

3. Bake for 20 to 25 minutes until the cheese is nicely melted and the onions are cooked.

4. Add fresh thyme or basil for garnish. Serve warm.

MAKES 4 SERVINGS

VARIATIONS

MEXICANA
Layer the crust with low-fat refried beans, salsa, and Monterey Jack cheese. Bake. Then top with fresh avocado and diced tomato.

FALL NIGHT
Brush the crust with olive oil, then layer arugula, mushrooms, and shredded smoked Gouda. Bake. Sprinkle with freshly chopped thyme and goat cheese. This is great on a chilly night.

CAPRI
Spread the crust with our homemade **Italian Holiday Tomato Sauce** (see p. 19). Top with black olives, capers, tuna, and crumbled feta, sprinkled with dried oregano and Parmesan cheese. Bake.

THANKSGIVING TREAT
Brush the crust with olive oil and layer with roasted, thinly sliced butternut squash, some fried sage leaves, blue cheese, and crumbled walnuts. Top with grated Parmesan and cracked black pepper. Bake.

NADIA'S PERSIAN CHICKEN

Pomegranate Reduction

Boil 1 cup (250 mL) pomegranate juice until it is reduced to 2 Tbsp (30 mL)—it will be thick and sugary, very tangy and sour.

My friend Nadia is one of the best cooks I know—when she puts her mind to it! She whips up the most delicious Persian dishes and manages to look eternally fabulous doing so. This is one of her favorites, and if you are lucky enough to be invited to her house, you are in for a real treat. But if not, I'm giving you a recipe that she has kept secret for many years . . .

½ cup (125 mL) pistachios
6 Tbsp (90 mL) olive oil, divided
2 large onions, thinly sliced
2 lb (900 g) chicken thighs and legs (skin-on, bone-in), cut up
1 cup (250 mL) cubed carrots
1 cup (250 mL) prunes, chopped
4 cups (1 L) pure pomegranate juice, divided
2 Tbsp (30 mL) pomegranate reduction (see sidebar)

1 tsp (5 mL) salt
½ tsp (2.5 mL) cracked black pepper
½ tsp (2.5 mL) ground turmeric
½ tsp (2.5 mL) ground cinnamon
2 Tbsp (30 mL) brown sugar or maple syrup
¼ cup (60 mL) walnuts for garnish
¼ cup (60 mL) pomegranate seeds for garnish

1. Preheat the oven to 350°F (175°C) and toast the pistachios until they begin to golden a little, about 3 to 5 minutes.

2. In a large heavy-bottomed skillet/pan, sauté the onions in 3 Tbsp (45 mL) olive oil until the onions are soft and translucent. Remove from pan with a slotted spoon and set aside.

3. Add the rest of the olive oil to the pan and add the chicken, browning well. Add the carrots and prunes and cook for another 2 to 3 minutes, stirring well. Remove skillet from heat.

4. Place the toasted pistachios in a food processor with the cooked onions and grind well. Add 1 cup (250 mL) of the pomegranate juice, the pomegranate reduction, salt, pepper, turmeric, cinnamon, and brown sugar, and pulse into a paste.

5. Add the creamy pistachio paste and the rest of the pomegranate juice to the chicken mixture, stirring gently. Cover and cook on low heat for 75 to 90 minutes, stirring occasionally so the nuts do not burn.

6. The sauce should be very creamy and have a sweet and sour taste. If too thick, add a bit more juice, and if too sour, add a bit more brown sugar or maple syrup. Transfer to a deep casserole dish to keep warm.

7. Garnish with the walnuts and pomegranate seeds.

MAKES 4 TO 6 SERVINGS

NOTE: Serve with basmati rice cooked with chicken stock, a little saffron, and lemon zest.

OLIVE ROASTED CHICKEN

This is a salty, savory dish that's perfect with a simple green salad or a toasted rice pilaf. It's great fresh out of the oven or used in wraps or sandwiches the next day.

4 skinless, boneless chicken breasts
1 Tbsp (15 mL) olive oil
4 Tbsp (60 mL) **Olive Pesto** (recipe follows)

Fresh basil for garnish
Handful toasted pine nuts for garnish (see p. 24)

1. Preheat the oven to 400°F (200°C).

2. Put the chicken breasts in a large casserole dish or roasting pan. Brush each piece of chicken with olive oil. Place 1 Tbsp (15 mL) **Olive Pesto** on each and spread evenly with the back of a spoon or a knife.

3. Cook for 30 minutes until clear juices run out of the thickest part of the meat.

4. Garnish with fresh basil and a handful of toasted pine nuts.

MAKES 4 SERVINGS

OLIVE PESTO

¾ cup (185 mL) Kalamata olives, chopped (green olives would be good too)
2 cloves garlic, crushed
⅓ cup (80 mL) toasted pine nuts (see p. 24)

3 Tbsp (45 mL) Parmesan cheese
¼ cup (60 mL) extra virgin olive oil
¼ cup (60 mL) chopped fresh basil

1. In a food processor, combine the olives, garlic, pine nuts, Parmesan cheese, olive oil, and basil. Blend until you have a coarse paste.

MAKES ¾ TO 1 CUP (185 TO 250 ML)

HIGH FIVES

GLUTEN-FREE RECIPES WITH FIVE INGREDIENTS OR LESS

This is something I came up with for my cooking show *He Said, She Said with Ken and Mary Jo*. I wanted to give viewers really simple recipes with five ingredients or less. People loved it when my co-host Ken Kostick and I used to fight over who had the best dish each show. I was the judge, so I pretty much won every time. We also made a rule, after 50 episodes, that stock, olive oil, and salt and pepper would be freebies and not count in the ingredients total. So it's the least I can do for all my gluten-free friends in their quest for the perfect, easy, delicious dish.

RECIPES

THE EASIEST BROCCOLI SOUP EVER

I have my friend Kenny to thank for this one—he lives in LA with his lovely wife Regan and is totally vegan. I'd heard about his magical soup and had some the other night. It was sublime—fresh, simple, and delicious. This is how he did it . . .

    PS. My daughter Lola is eating it right now.

2 broccoli heads, chopped
7 cups (1.75 L) gluten-free
    vegetable or chicken stock
    (or enough to cover broccoli
    in a large pot)
1½ lemons, juiced

1 tsp (5 mL) salt + extra for
    seasoning
1 tsp (5 mL) ground cumin
    (see note)
½ cup (125 mL) olive oil
Pepper to taste

Why not try . . . some great garnishes! I know Kenny would not like this, but garnish each bowl of soup with a dollop of Greek yogurt and crumbled bacon.

Or try crumbled corn chips or toasted corn tortillas with a dollop of guacamole.

1. In a large pot, cover the broccoli with stock, about 7 cups (1.75 L). Add the lemon juice and about 1 tsp (5 mL) salt.

2. Bring to a boil and reduce to medium heat until the broccoli is cooked, about 18 to 20 minutes, and the stock starts to thicken. Set aside to cool the broth.

3. Put the cooled broth and broccoli into a food processor and blend until the mixture begins to combine. Taste and season, and add the ground cumin. You can also add more lemon juice if you like.

4. With the food processor running, slowly add the olive oil. It thickens up the soup and it will become creamy. Taste again and season.

MAKES 7 TO 8 CUPS (1.75 TO 2 L)

NOTE: Dried herbs are optional to give the flavor you like. I am using cumin for this recipe, but you could try a little turmeric or a touch of dill.

ONE POT MIRACLE

This is a great easy meal that is especially cozy on a chilly fall night. It's also good when you're pressed for time or having people over at the last minute. This is a basic recipe but you can always substitute, throwing in some of your own personal favorites. Open a nice bottle of wine and enjoy.

Why not try...
adding olives instead of sundried tomatoes, and fresh basil to finish the dish?

4 chicken breasts, skin-on, bone-in
2 Tbsp (30 mL) olive oil
1 red pepper, julienned
¼ cup (60 mL) sundried tomatoes, chopped
1½ cups (375 mL) uncooked rice (arborio rice works best)
3 cups (750 mL) gluten-free chicken stock
¾ cup (185 mL) chopped fresh Italian parsley
Salt and cracked black pepper to taste

1. In a large heavy-bottom pot, brown the chicken in the olive oil (remember, this is a "free" ingredient) over medium-high heat, about 2 to 3 minutes per side, seasoning both sides with salt and pepper. You want the chicken to be a nice golden-brown color.

2. Add the red pepper and sauté until it starts to soften, about 1 to 2 minutes.

3. Add the sundried tomatoes and rice and combine with the other ingredients, browning the rice slightly.

4. Add the chicken stock (another free ingredient) and bring to a boil, then reduce to medium-low heat and continue cooking until the rice and chicken are cooked, approx. 25 to 35 minutes, checking occasionally and stirring the rice so it does not stick.

5. Serve it straight out of the pot or on a platter. Garnish with the fresh parsley and lots of salt and cracked black pepper.

MAKES 4 SERVINGS

LIME FRESH TACOS

Why not try...some
shredded iceberg lettuce, diced
tomatoes, black beans, and
my Avocado Foam (see p. 41)?
You can also add shredded raw
cheese, sour cream, or ground
walnuts for garnishes.

This recipe is built on some of the staples I know will make your life easier—and one of the stars is shredded chicken. Always make sure you have some in your refrigerator or freezer. It will make everything seem manageable. I just cooked it for 20 people at a family dinner and it was gone in seconds.

1 medium onion, finely chopped
6 Tbsp (90 mL) olive oil, divided
1½ cups (375 mL) julienned red pepper
3 to 3½ cups (750 to 875 mL) shredded chicken (see p. 44)
Salt and pepper to taste

2 limes, juiced
½ cup (125 mL) fresh cilantro, chopped
8 to 10 corn tortillas (crunchy or soft depending on preference)

1. In a large heavy skillet over medium heat, sauté the onions in 1 Tbsp (15 mL) olive oil until soft, approx. 3 to 5 minutes. Then add the red pepper and cook for another 3 to 4 minutes.

2. Add the chicken and coat well with 3 Tbsp (45 mL) olive oil and the onion-pepper mixture. Salt and pepper to taste and sauté for approx. 2 to 3 minutes.

3. Add the lime juice and sauté for another 1 to 2 minutes.

4. Mix in the fresh cilantro and the remaining 2 Tbsp (30 mL) olive oil and serve immediately in corn tortillas or over greens.

MAKES 8 TO 10 TACOS

NOTE: I play around with the olive oil. Sometimes I need to add more than 2 Tbsp (30 mL) at the end—see what works for you!

GOLDEN BEET SALAD

I love beets—especially in the summer, fresh from the garden. They're so sweet and beautiful in many dishes. This is one of my mom's favorite salads—and I have to agree it's sublime.

2 cups (500 mL) chopped
  golden beets
4 Tbsp (60 mL) olive oil, divided
Salt and pepper to taste
1 cup (250 mL) pecans

2 Tbsp (30 mL) brown sugar
4 cups (1 L) arugula
½ cup (125 mL) crumbled goat
  cheese

1. Preheat your oven to 400°F (200°C). Toss the uncooked beets in 2 Tbsp (30 mL) olive oil and salt and pepper. Place on a non-stick baking sheet and cook for 35 to 40 minutes turning twice with a spatula. Remove and set aside.

2. Toss the pecans in 1 tsp (5 mL) olive oil and the brown sugar and place on a baking sheet with waxed paper or aluminum foil. Bake in a 375°F (190°C) oven for about 6 to 8 minutes until the nuts start to get golden.

3. In a bowl, combine the cooked beets, toasted pecans, arugula, and crumbled goat cheese. Douse with the rest of the olive oil and season with salt and pepper. Give it a good toss and serve.

MAKES 4 SERVINGS

Amp it up!

Turn your salad into a main course with the addition of lemon-grilled chicken. Marinate skinless, boneless chicken breasts in lots of olive oil, lemon juice, and salt and pepper. Grill or bake in a 385°F (195°C) oven for 40 to 50 minutes until done. Serve over the arugula and beet salad.

ROASTED PINE NUT PILAF

Why not try ...garnishing with shredded carrots and raisins for a more exotic dish? Or try some chopped fresh Italian parsley. Fresh mint is great too.

I am a rice fanatic. I always have been—jasmine, sticky, brown, risotto—I love it all. This is an easy, comforting pilaf that would be great with a roast chicken or something more exotic like curry or an Indian lamb dish.

1 small onion, finely diced
2 Tbsp (30 mL) olive oil
Salt and pepper to taste
1½ cups (375 mL) uncooked
   rice, jasmine or basmati
½ tsp (2.5 mL) ground turmeric
2½ cups (625 mL) gluten-free
   chicken or veggie stock

½ cup (125 mL) fresh
   orange juice
½ cup (125 mL) toasted pine
   nuts (see p. 24)
2 tsp (10 mL) orange zest
   (optional)
Cracked black pepper for
   garnish

1. In a medium saucepan, sauté the onions in the olive oil until the onions soften, 3 to 5 minutes, and season with salt and pepper.

2. Add the rice and cook, stirring constantly, until it starts to golden, about 3 to 5 minutes. You want it to have a little color.

3. Coat the rice mixture with the turmeric.

4. Add the stock and the orange juice and bring to a boil. Turn the heat down to a medium simmer and cook until the rice is done, about 15 to 18 minutes, depending on the kind of rice you use.

5. When the rice is cooked, serve on a platter and sprinkle the toasted pine nuts and orange zest on top with lots of cracked black pepper.

MAKES 6 SERVINGS

CITRUS HUMMUS

If you're going gluten-free, you're required to eat hummus! High in protein, simple to make, and great in salads, sandwiches, and on its own, it is a basic that you can modify and personalize to your taste. I make it without garlic (believe it or not) for a fresher taste.

One 19 oz (540 mL) can
    chickpeas, drained
1 lemon, juiced
Zest of ½ lemon
2 Tbsp (30 mL) tahini sauce

¼ cup (60 mL) gluten-free
    tamari sauce
1 tsp (5 mL) ground cumin
¼ cup (60 mL) olive oil
Salt and pepper to taste

Why not try...using lime or orange juice instead of lemon? Throw in some sundried tomatoes, olives, or roasted red peppers. Add a little fresh basil or coriander for a different flavor. There are a lot of ways to make hummus. Experiment!

1. In a food processor, blend chickpeas, lemon juice and zest, tahini sauce, tamari sauce, ground cumin, olive oil, and salt and pepper to taste. Blend until you have a creamy paste.

MAKES APPROX. 2 CUPS (500 ML)

KALE MAGIC

I know kale is very trendy right now, but I love it anyway. Cooked or in a salad, it adds a zing to everyday dishes and is beyond good for you. This is a salad I had at the Soho Club in Los Angeles during a very important business meeting, and I just made it for Billy Bush and Kit Hoover on *Access Hollywood Live*. I have made it super easy for you.

½ cup (125 mL) uncooked
   quinoa
4 cups (1 L) kale, julienned
   (I love Tuscan kale)
2 to 3 Tbsp (30 to 45 mL) olive
   oil, to taste

½ lemon, juiced
2 avocados, diced
½ cup (125 mL) pistachios
Salt and pepper to taste

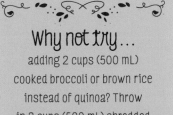

Why not try...
adding 2 cups (500 mL)
cooked broccoli or brown rice
instead of quinoa? Throw
in 2 cups (500 mL) shredded
chicken (see p. 44) and you are
in protein city. Experiment.

1. Cook quinoa in 1 cup (250 mL) water according to the instructions on the package. Set aside.

2. In a large bowl, toss the kale with a little olive oil and the lemon juice to soften the kale. Add the avocado and quinoa, and toss again. Finish off with a little more olive oil, the pistachios, and lots of salt and pepper to taste.

MAKES 4 SERVINGS

GINGER MASH

Why not try ...adding
some wasabi mustard and
fresh cilantro for more of
an Asian feel, and serve it
with roasted pork.

Sweet potatoes are one of the most perfect foods, high in vitamins and totally versatile. I love them baked, fried, mashed, or puréed, in soups and in salads. This is a quick way to get a whole bunch of flavor in a short time.

4 cups (1 L) chopped sweet
potatoes, all the same size
2 tsp (10 mL) finely shredded
fresh ginger
¼ cup (60 mL) butter

2 Tbsp (30 mL) brown sugar
½ cup (125 mL) cream cheese
Ground cinnamon for garnish
(optional)

1. In a large pot of boiling water, cook the sweet potatoes and shredded ginger until they are done and fall off the fork. Drain most of the water but reserve about ½ to ¾ cup (125 to 185 mL) in a separate bowl. Then mash up the sweet potatoes and ginger.

2. Over low heat while the potatoes are still hot, mix in the butter and the sugar until all the ingredients are incorporated. Add as much reserved sweet potato stock as needed to blend—usually about ½ cup (125 mL), depending on how thick you like it.

3. Finish by mixing in the cream cheese.

4. Garnish with a sprinkling of ground cinnamon, if desired.

MAKES 4 TO 6 SERVINGS

LEMON HEAVEN

What is better than a nice lemony broth filled with noodles? Here is an easy version for inspiration and some afternoon calm.

2 to 4 oz (60 to 110 g) dried gluten-free noodles (rice, quinoa, whatever you like)
½ cup (125 mL) chopped shallots
2 Tbsp (30 mL) olive oil
Salt and pepper to taste

6 cups (1.5 L) gluten-free chicken stock
2 lemons, juiced
½ cup (125 mL) chopped green onions
½ cup (125 mL) grated Parmesan cheese

1. Cook noodles in a large pot of salted, boiling water until al dente. Drain and set aside.

2. In a large soup pot, sauté the shallots in the olive oil until soft. Season with salt and pepper. Add the stock and lemon juice and bring to a boil.

3. Reduce to medium heat and cook for 10 to 12 minutes. Add the cooked noodles (or quinoa or rice, if using) and cook for another 2 to 3 minutes.

4. Add the green onions and Parmesan cheese, stirring it all in for another 2 to 3 minutes. Salt and pepper to taste.

MAKES 4 SERVINGS

Amp it up!

You can do lots of things with this basic broth. Add 1 cup (250 mL) broccoli and some shredded chicken (see p. 44) for a heavier meal.

You can also use only one lemon and add some ginger or lemongrass for a Thai taste. Throw in some spinach, shrimp, and lots of fresh cilantro and basil. Garnish with some salted peanuts.

Why not try ...rice or quinoa instead of noodles?

I CAN HAVE PASTA? SWEET!

The hardest thing about gluten-free eating is that sometimes you might feel excluded from all the good stuff. That was a real concern for me, especially going gluten-free with an eight-year-old girl and a teenage boy. It is important to know that you can eat well and have things that you love delivered in a different package. Find a brand of gluten-free pasta that you like—rice, corn, quinoa-based—and embrace it. Then start to have fun as you realize your culinary life is just beginning, not ending.

When cooking gluten-free pasta, pay close attention to the instructions and the cooking time. It's often different from regular pasta, and if overcooked can become very mushy. It might take a few tries to find the pasta that best suits your needs but don't worry—there are tons of great brands.

For every recipe I have given the pasta amount to be 1 lb (450 g) dried. When you mix linguine, spaghetti, and fettucine, always hold back about 2 oz (60 g) cooked pasta until you mix in your sauce to see what ratio of sauce to pasta you like!

RECIPES

LINGUINE WITH LEMON TUNA CREAM

This to me is the ultimate comfort pasta—like a mini tuna casserole. I like it really lemony with lots of dill. I tested this on Jack and his friends and I got the thumbs-up from six teenagers—that's a major endorsement! I think . . .

1 lb (450 g) dried gluten-free linguine

1½ cups (375 mL) half-and-half cream

1½ cups (375 mL) gluten-free chicken stock

1 Tbsp (15 mL) finely shredded lemon zest

¼ cup (60 mL) lemon juice

¾ cup (185 mL) finely grated Parmesan cheese + extra for garnish

Two 6 oz (170 g) cans white tuna, well drained

⅓ cup (80 mL) capers

¼ cup (60 mL) chopped fresh dill

Salt and cracked black pepper to taste

Grated Parmesan for garnish

Why not try . . . using shredded chicken (see p. 44) instead of tuna, and throw in some fresh chilies for heat? Or try adding 1 or 2 cups (250 to 500 mL) mushrooms.

Or if you want to lower the fat content, use only ½ cup (125 mL) cream and add more stock for a lighter flavor.

1. Cook the pasta in a large pot of salted, boiling water until al dente (check instructions on package). Drain and set aside.

2. In a large deep pan, put the cream, the stock, and the lemon zest. Cook on medium heat and allow to simmer for about 3 to 4 minutes.

3. Add the lemon juice, gradually whisking it in, then add the Parmesan cheese, being careful that the sauce does not separate. Cook for 3 to 5 minutes, until it starts to thicken.

4. Add the tuna and the capers and cook until it starts to thicken a bit more—2 to 3 minutes.

5. Add the pasta to the sauce and toss with fresh dill. Garnish with more Parmesan cheese. Top with lots of cracked black pepper and salt to taste.

MAKES 4 TO 6 SERVINGS

WATERCRESS AND WALNUT PASTA

This is a great go-to pasta, winter, summer or fall. The sweet pears with the tang of blue cheese and fresh lemon zest make it an unusual savory combination. I love blue cheese but if you don't care for it, add some goat cheese or feta. Or use apples and pecans—be creative and make it your own.

Why not try ... serving this without pasta? Add more greens with grilled chicken breasts—and it's dinner!

Or if you want it to contain less fat, use turkey bacon. Be sure to compensate with 1 Tbsp (15 mL) or so of olive oil when you toss the pasta and greens.

---

1 lb (450 g) dried gluten-free rotini

2 cups (500 mL) chopped watercress

1 cup (250 mL) chopped arugula

¾ cup (185 mL) chopped bacon

½ cup (125 mL) finely chopped shallots

2 pears, sliced about ¼ inch (6 mm) thick

3 Tbsp (45 mL) balsamic vinegar

3 Tbsp (45 mL) brown sugar

½ lemon, juiced

1 tsp (5 mL) shredded lemon zest

1 cup (250 mL) crumbled organic blue, feta, or goat cheese

¾ cup (185 mL) walnuts

Fresh Italian parsley for garnish

Dried cranberries for garnish

---

1. In a large pot of boiling, salted water, cook the pasta until al dente, usually about 8 to 10 minutes for gluten-free (but read the package instructions to be sure).

2. Wash and dry the watercress and arugula.

3. In a medium pan, cook the bacon and shallots over medium heat until the bacon is almost crisp.

4. Add pear slices, balsamic vinegar, brown sugar, lemon juice and zest, and cook until the pears are soft, about 3 to 5 minutes.

5. In a large mixing bowl, combine the pasta, the greens, the pear mixture, the crumbled cheese, and the walnuts and toss well. So yummy!

6. Serve on a large platter and garnish with a little fresh Italian parsley and some dried cranberries.

MAKES 4 TO 6 SERVINGS

OLIVE AND PINE NUT PASTA

Why not try...zucchini or spaghetti squash as a base, instead of traditional pasta? Use uncooked zucchini and cut it with a tool called a julienner. It will shred it like spaghetti. Try some **Basil Cashew Pesto** (see p. 20) with it. It is sublime! The squash should be cooked and then shredded with a fork. It is delicious with a little olive oil, fresh herbs, and Parmesan cheese, or try **Italian Holiday Tomato Sauce** (see p. 19) for a fresh, but still filling "pasta" dinner.

This is a simple and very savory pasta, perfect for a chilly night watching *House Hunters* and wishing you lived somewhere else.

1 lb (450 g) package dried gluten-free spaghetti
3 Tbsp (45 mL) olive oil, divided
3 cloves garlic, minced
1 cup (250 mL) Kalamata olives
⅓ cup (80 mL) capers
2 Tbsp (30 mL) chopped fresh thyme

2 Tbsp (30 mL) shredded fresh lemon zest
Cracked black pepper to taste
½ cup (125 mL) chopped fresh Italian parsley
½ cup (125 mL) toasted pine nuts (see p. 24)
Freshly grated Parmesan cheese

1. In a large pot of salted, boiling water, cook the pasta until al dente, about 10 to 12 minutes. Drain and set aside.

2. In a large sauté pan over medium heat, add 2 Tbsp (30 mL) olive oil and toast the garlic until golden. Be careful not to burn it.

3. Add the olives, capers, fresh thyme, and lemon zest. Sauté well for about 3 to 4 minutes, until the olives are warmed through. Cover liberally with cracked black pepper.

4. Toss in the cooked pasta and add remaining 1 Tbsp (15 mL) olive oil.

5. Toss in the fresh parsley and pine nuts, and serve with freshly grated Parmesan.

MAKES 4 SERVINGS

ROASTED CHERRY TOMATOES AND PANCETTA PASTA

(OR AS I CALL IT, BLT PASTA)

I am infatuated with roasted cherry tomatoes. I use them in everything. All you do is roast them at a low to medium heat with lots of salt. I usually do them at 350°F (175°C) for 40 to 50 minutes and they come out chewy, sweet, and a little tart (just like me!). Make up a whole batch and keep them on-hand to spice up salads, sauces, and pastas.

Why not try...
adding roasted red peppers or grilled eggplant instead of tomatoes? You can always throw in some black olives or a handful of arugula for punch.

3 cups (750 mL) cherry tomatoes (you can always use the extras later)

Kosher salt to taste

1 lb (450 g) package dried gluten-free penne

12 slices pancetta (reserve 4 for a garnish) or 7 to 8 slices bacon (2 for garnish)

1 cup (250 mL) crumbled goat cheese

½ cup (125 mL) chopped fresh basil

½ cup (125 mL) chopped fresh Italian parsley

Cracked black pepper to taste

1. Preheat your oven to 350°F (175°C). Line up the cherry tomatoes on a non-stick baking sheet. Sprinkle the tomatoes with lots of salt. Roast approx. 40 to 50 minutes, until the tomatoes lose their moisture and become chewy.

2. In a large pot of salted boiling water, cook the penne al dente, according to instructions on package.

3. In a small pan, fry up 4 pieces of pancetta or 2 pieces of bacon until they become crispy. Set aside for garnish.

4. In a large frying pan, cook the rest of the pancetta or bacon until crispy.

5. Remove the pancetta or bacon and save about 1 Tbsp (15 mL) fat to toss the pasta with. Crumble the pancetta or bacon into little pieces.

6. In a bowl, toss the roasted tomatoes, pancetta, pasta, basil, parsley, reserved fat, and goat cheese.

7. Finish off with lots of cracked black pepper and crumbled bits of pancetta or bacon garnish. This is the most delicious, easiest pasta ever.

MAKES 4 TO 6 SERVINGS

LIME NOODLES WITH FRIED GREEN ONIONS

Why not try...

adding some beef tenderloin
or shrimp? Try garnishing
with toasted sesame seeds
and toasted coconut.

This is a fresh dish that can put an exotic twist on a boring
Tuesday dinner.

1 lb (450 g) dried gluten-free
    linguine or fettuccine
1½ cup (375 mL) chopped
    green onions, divided
One 14 oz (398 mL) can
    unsweetened coconut milk
½ cup (125 mL) fresh basil
¾ cup (185 mL) fresh cilantro,
    divided
2 cups (500 mL) fresh spinach
1 clove garlic, minced
¼ cup (60 mL) gluten-free
    tamari sauce
3 Tbsp (45 mL) **Hoisin For Days**
    sauce (see p. 25)

3 limes, juiced, divided
1 Tbsp (15 mL) olive oil
2 Tbsp (30 mL) sesame oil
½ cup (125 mL) shallots,
    chopped
½ cup (125 mL) sliced oyster or
    shitake mushrooms
2 cups (500 mL) shredded
    chicken (see p. 44)
½ red pepper, julienned
Chili flakes to taste (optional)
½ cup (125 mL) salted peanuts
Cracked black pepper for
    garnish
Lime zest for garnish

1. Cook pasta in a large pot of boiling, salted water, until al dente (check instructions on package). Drain and set aside.

2. In a food processor, combine ½ cup (125 mL) green onions, coconut milk, basil, ¼ cup (60 mL) cilantro, spinach, garlic, tamari sauce, hoisin sauce, and the juice of 2 limes. Blend until smooth.

3. In a large frying pan, fry the shallots and the remaining 1 cup (250 mL) green onions in the olive oil and sesame oil until they start to brown. Add the mushrooms and sauté for another 2 minutes.

4. Add the chicken, red pepper, chili flakes, and the rest of the lime juice and sauté for 3 to 4 minutes.

5. Add the sauce from the food processor and cook for another 3 to 5 minutes. Toss the pasta in just before serving and arrange on a large platter.

6. Garnish with salted peanuts, cracked black pepper, lime zest, and the remaining ½ cup (125 mL) fresh cilantro, finely chopped.

MAKES 4 TO 6 SERVINGS

SWEET POTATO MACARONI

This dish is a version of traditional macaroni and cheese—I have snuck in some fruits and veggies that should get by the most discerning palate. It has been kid-tested—and they loved it. They even asked for seconds...

Why not try...pumpkin or butternut squash instead of the sweet potato? You could also use arborio rice as your base, or to make it lower fat, use more stock and cream.

4 cups (1 L) dried gluten-free macaroni
2½ sweet potatoes
3 Tbsp (45 mL) butter
½ cup (125 mL) finely chopped celery
1 cup (250 mL) cubed apple (tart, like Granny Smith)
1 cup (250 mL) chopped onions
Salt and pepper to taste
¾ cup (185 mL) half-and-half cream

1 cup (250 mL) gluten-free chicken or veggie stock
1 cup (250 mL) freshly grated Parmesan cheese + extra for garnish
1 cup (250 mL) freshly grated, raw sharp cheddar or Gruyère cheese
½ cup (125 mL) chopped fresh parsley
½ tsp (2.5 mL) ground nutmeg
½ cup (125 mL) chopped pistachios

1. Cook pasta in a large pot of boiling, salted water, until al dente (check instructions on package). Drain and set aside.

2. Cut sweet potatoes into 1-inch (2.5 cm) cubes and cook them in boiling salted water until soft. This should yield approx. 2 cups (500 mL) cubed potatoes.

3. In a medium pan, sauté in butter the celery, apple, and onions until soft, about 3 to 5 minutes. Salt and pepper to taste. Add the sweet potato and sauté for another 1 to 2 minutes.

4. In a large bowl, combine the pasta, the sweet potato mixture, cream, stock, Parmesan cheese, cheddar or Gruyère, parsley, ground nutmeg, and salt and pepper. Mix well.

5. In a medium greased baking dish, spread the mixture evenly. Sprinkle the pistachios on top and bake at 385°F (195°C) for 25 to 30 minutes until everything is melted and bubbly. Top with extra Parmesan.

MAKES 6 SERVINGS

PUMPKIN PASTA WITH TOASTED PECANS

This pasta reminds me of holidays, huddling around fireplaces and eating loads of comfort food. This dish is perfect with a green salad and lots of wine. Serve warm and enjoy with the company of good friends . . .

1 lb (450 g) dried gluten-free penne
¾ cup (185 mL) chopped sweet onion
2 cloves garlic, minced
1 Tbsp (15 mL) butter
1 Tbsp (15 mL) olive oil
1 Tbsp (15 mL) shredded fresh sage leaves
½ cup (125 mL) dates, chopped
¼ cup (60 mL) port
One 15 oz (425 mL) can pumpkin purée
1 cup (250 mL) gluten-free chicken stock
¼ cup (60 mL) coconut milk
½ tsp (2.5 mL) ground nutmeg
½ tsp (2.5 mL) ground cinnamon
2 Tbsp (30 mL) maple syrup
½ cup (125 mL) cream cheese
2 Tbsp (30 mL) fresh rosemary
½ cup (125 mL) toasted pecans (see p. 24)
Cracked black pepper for garnish
Freshly grated Parmesan cheese for garnish

1. In a large pot of boiling, salted water, cook the pasta until al dente (check instructions on package). Drain and set aside.

2. In a large pan, sauté the onions and garlic in the butter and olive oil until the garlic starts to turn a little golden.

3. Add the sage and sauté for another minute. Then add the dates and cook for an additional 2 to 3 minutes.

4. Deglaze the pan with the port and sauté for another minute.

5. Add the pumpkin purée, stock, coconut milk, ground nutmeg, ground cinnamon, and maple syrup and cook for another 3 to 4 minutes, until the sauce thickens.

6. Add the cream cheese and stir until all the cheese is blended into the sauce.

7. Add the pasta to the sauce and mix well. Add the rosemary and toss again.

8. Serve on a large platter garnished with the toasted pecans and lots of cracked black pepper. Grate fresh Parmesan cheese on every serving.

MAKES 4 SERVINGS

MUSHROOM CREAM PASTA

Why not try ... adding ¼ cup (60 mL) chopped dates or apricots? Instead of the thyme, try rosemary, and if you want to omit the cream, you can use some gluten-free stock and wine. Just increase the Parmesan cheese to 1 cup (250 mL) if you take this route, so it won't be too runny.

This is the favorite pasta of most of my friends. It's creamy, rich, and full of mushrooms and alcohol. What's not to like?

1 lb (450 g) dried gluten-free fettuccine
½ cup (125 mL) chopped shallots
3 Tbsp (45 mL) butter
4 cups (1 L) assorted mushrooms, chopped
1 tsp (5 mL) salt (approx.)
1 tsp (5 mL) crack black pepper (approx.)
½ cup (125 mL) port

2 Tbsp (30 mL) chopped fresh thyme
1½ cups (375 mL) half-and-half cream
½ tsp (2.5 mL) ground nutmeg
½ tsp (2.5 mL) ground cinnamon
¾ cup (185 mL) grated Parmesan cheese, divided
⅓ cup (80 mL) pecans, chopped
½ cup (125 mL) fresh Italian parsley, chopped

1. Cook pasta in a large pot of boiling, salted water, until al dente (check instructions on the package). Drain and set aside.

2. In a large saucepan, sauté the shallots in the butter over medium heat until soft.

3. Add mushrooms and salt and pepper and sauté until the mushrooms start to absorb some of the liquid, about 4 to 5 minutes.

4. Add the port and thyme, cooking until the mushrooms absorb most of the liquid.

5. Reduce the heat to low and stir in the cream, ground nutmeg, ground cinnamon, and ¼ cup (60 mL) Parmesan cheese. Cook until the sauce starts to thicken slightly.

6. Add the pasta to the sauce and coat well. Mix in the additional Parmesan cheese and the pecans. Transfer to a platter or bowl and garnish with the chopped fresh parsley.

MAKES 4 TO 6 SERVINGS

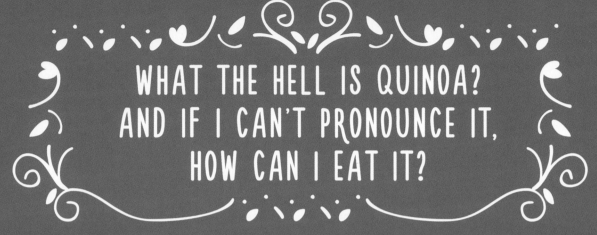

WHAT THE HELL IS QUINOA? AND IF I CAN'T PRONOUNCE IT, HOW CAN I EAT IT?

(PLUS A FEW OTHER GRAINS I HAVE THROWN IN)

Simply put, quinoa is the "It Girl" of the gluten-free movement. It is the Holy Grail of nutrition that everyone wants to get to know and master. If she were on match.com (I'm giving quinoa female characteristics because she seems pretty kick-ass to me— like a lot of women I know), she would list her qualities as:

"I strive to be one of the most perfect proteins possible, and even though I can look and taste like a grain, I am not. I'm actually related more to the spinach and chard family (don't ask!) and the part you all desire is actually a seed, which when cooked has a delicious nutty taste and falls somewhere in texture between rice and couscous. Not to brag, but I contain heart-healthy fats that kick most of my grain counterparts to the curb. I also am known for my anti-inflammatory benefits and the term 'antioxidant' has been attached to my wagon a time or two. Right now, I am looking for someone who is open to good health, not averse to trying new recipes where I have a starring role, and in it for the long term. I know one day my "It Girl" status may fade, but someone who really appreciates me will know my benefits are lifelong. I also like long walks on the beach and NFL football. Skeptics and narrow-minded people need not apply."

RECIPES

MEDITERRANEAN MADNESS

This quinoa dish has a fresh but exotic vibe that will please all your customers. The secret is the tahini in the dressing that gives it a richer flavor.

2 cups (500 mL) uncooked quinoa
1½ cups (375 mL) diced tomatoes
½ cup (125 mL) diced red onion
1 cup (250 mL) diced and seeded Persian cucumbers
½ cup (125 mL) diced celery
½ cup (125 mL) fresh Italian parsley, chopped
½ cup (125 mL) fresh mint, chopped
½ cup (125 mL) fresh cilantro, chopped
Salt and pepper to taste

DRESSING:
1 lime, juiced
¼ cup (60 mL) olive oil
2 Tbsp (30 mL) tahini sauce
2 Tbsp (30 mL) gluten-free tamari sauce
Salt and pepper to taste

½ cup (125 mL) smoked almonds, crushed, for garnish
Cracked black pepper for garnish

Why not try ...wrapping the quinoa in a rice or corn wrap? Throw in fresh avocado, some hummus, and call it lunch.

1. Cook the quinoa according to the instructions on the package and set aside.

2. In a large mixing bowl, combine cooked quinoa, tomatoes, onion, cucumbers, celery, parsley, mint, and cilantro. Season with salt and pepper and mix well.

3. In a smaller bowl, combine lime juice, olive oil, tahini sauce, tamari sauce, and salt and pepper to taste. Pour about two-thirds of the dressing over the quinoa mixture and toss well. I like a lot of dressing but some prefer a drier salad. See which suits you better—you can always use the rest of the dressing on another salad or save it for later.

4. Serve on a large platter and sprinkle with smoked almonds and lots of cracked pepper.

MAKES 9 TO 10 CUPS (2.25 TO 2.5 L)

GREEN ONION AND QUINOA OMELET

Why not try…

using roasted red peppers and shallots instead of the green onions? Or try mushrooms, spinach, and Swiss cheese.

This is a good basic frittata using quinoa as its base. This recipe has green onions and goat cheese but feel free to experiment using some of the ideas in the sidebar. This recipe reminds me of the Chinese spring pancakes I used to get for dim sum when I was a little girl. Make it a bit more Asian with plum dipping sauce or some sweet Thai chili sauce.

½ cup (125 mL) uncooked quinoa
6 eggs
½ tsp (2.5 mL) salt
½ tsp (2.5 mL) pepper
2 cups (500 mL) chopped fresh green onion

2 Tbsp (30 mL) olive oil
½ cup (125 mL) chopped fresh Italian parsley
¾ cup (185 mL) goat cheese or ricotta

1. Preheat the oven to 500°F (260°C).

2. Cook the quinoa according to the instructions on the package and set aside.

3. In a bowl, whisk together eggs, the cooked quinoa, salt, and pepper. Set aside.

4. In a large omelet pan, sauté the green onions in the olive oil until soft.

5. Add the egg and quinoa mixture to the pan and sprinkle with the Italian parsley. Gently scramble the eggs with a whisk, pulling at the sides and allowing the uncooked egg to spill over and cook. Once the omelet sets, sprinkle the goat cheese (or ricotta) on the egg mixture and allow it to cook for another minute or so.

6. Put the pan into the oven until the egg mixture cooks through and the goat cheese melts, usually a couple of minutes—but keep an eye on it!

7. Cut in wedges and serve with a fresh green salad.

MAKES 4 SERVINGS

BLACK BEAN AND QUINOA BURGERS

These burgers are the perfect alternative to meat. They are high in protein, substantial, and delicious. Great with a gluten-free bun or on top of a green salad, they totally pack a punch.

½ cup (125 mL) uncooked quinoa
¼ cup (60 mL) walnuts
One 19 oz (540 mL) can black beans, drained and rinsed
1 clove garlic, finely chopped
½ cup (125 mL) chopped onions
1 tsp (5 mL) prepared horseradish
¼ cup (60 mL) chopped red pepper
¼ cup (60 mL) gluten-free breadcrumbs
1 egg
¼ cup (60 mL) sundried tomatoes, chopped
2 scallions, chopped
Salt and pepper to taste
2 Tbsp (30 mL) olive oil
5 or 6 gluten-free hamburger buns
Sliced avocado for garnish
Arugula for garnish

Why not try . . . making the burgers with half corn and half black beans? Add some cilantro for a southwestern flavor, and serve with salsa and guacamole.

1. Cook quinoa according to the instructions on the package and set aside.

2. In a food processor, grind up the walnuts.

3. Add the beans to the food processor and pulse slightly, so the mixture is still chunky.

4. Transfer to a mixing bowl and add the quinoa, garlic, onions, horseradish, red pepper, breadcrumbs, egg, sundried tomatoes, and scallions. Mix well. Salt and pepper to taste.

5. Make into 5 or 6 burger patties, depending on the size you want.

6. In a large skillet over medium-high, heat the olive oil and cook the burgers for about 4 minutes per side, until the outside is golden and crispy.

7. Place inside hamburger buns and garnish with slices of avocado and arugula.

MAKES 5 TO 6 HAMBURGERS

ANNE'S ORGANIC APRICOT AND QUINOA SALAD

I have to admit, my friend Anne is a pretty great cook. She whipped this up one cottage weekend with about 10 lb (4.5 kg) pork tenderloin that she cooked in case anyone was hungry—like, there were four of us . . . Needless to say, she is an excellent host.

1½ cups (375 mL) uncooked quinoa
3 cups (750 mL) orange juice
1 cup (250 mL) chopped organic apricots

½ cup (125 mL) chopped fresh mint
Olive oil to toss
Sea salt and cracked black pepper to taste
1 tsp (5 mL) orange zest

1. Cook the quinoa in the orange juice, according to instructions on the package. Set aside.

2. In a bowl, combine the cooled cooked quinoa, apricots, and chopped fresh mint. Toss with a little olive oil, sea salt, and cracked black pepper.

3. Garnish with the orange zest.

MAKES 4 TO 6 SERVINGS

BUTTERNUT SQUASH AND QUINOA SALAD

This is such an easy salad but packed with nutrition and so delicious. You can have it for a healthy but substantial lunch, or as an appetizer for one of your great dinner parties. I just had it in Palm Springs, lounging by the pool and trying to forget that tomorrow was Monday and I had to make lunches . . .

¾ cups (185 mL) uncooked
  quinoa
2 cups (500 mL) cubed
  butternut squash (see note)
3 Tbsp (45 mL) olive oil, divided
Salt and pepper to taste
2 Tbsp (30 mL) brown sugar
  (optional)

4 cups (1 L) arugula
1 cup (250 mL) roughly
  chopped walnuts
½ cup (125 mL) dried
  cranberries
½ cup (125 mL) shaved
  Parmesan cheese
Cracked black pepper

1. Cook the quinoa according to the instructions on the package and set aside.

2. Spread the cubed squash on a baking dish with 1 Tbsp (15 mL) olive oil and salt and pepper. Bake in a 375°F (190°C) oven until done, about 30 to 35 minutes. You can add a little brown sugar to slightly caramelize the squash. Allow to cool.

3. Line a serving platter with the arugula.

4. In a bowl, mix together the quinoa, squash, walnuts, and cranberries. Toss with 2 Tbsp (30 mL) olive oil and lots of salt and pepper.

5. Spread the quinoa mixture over the arugula. Garnish with shaved Parmesan cheese and cracked black pepper.

MAKES 4 SERVINGS

NOTE: You can buy cubed squash ready to go!

Amp it up!

Top the salad with some shredded chicken (see p. 44) for an extra boost of protein.

Why not try . . .

pumpkin or sweet potato instead of squash? You can also use pecans and dried cherries instead of cranberries.

MY PARIS MOMENT MEATLOAF

I love Dijon mustard and cornichons more than almost anything. I have combined them with quinoa, ground turkey, and walnuts for a very delicious and healthy dish. Make it and pretend you are in Paris for the summer, about to make your way to St. Tropez for the weekend . . . Pack light and brag about your meatloaf! Okay . . . I think I need a vacation.

~~~~~~

¾ cup (185 mL) uncooked
  quinoa
1 onion, roughly chopped
1 stalk celery, roughly chopped
2 carrots, roughly chopped
2 cloves garlic
2 Tbsp (30 mL) olive oil
Salt and pepper to taste
2 cups (500 mL) kale or
  arugula, finely chopped

1½ lb (700 g) ground turkey
1 Tbsp (15 mL) prepared
  horseradish
2 Tbsp (30 mL) Dijon mustard
¼ cup (60 mL) ground walnuts
1 egg
½ cup (125 mL) cornichon
  pickles, diced
2 Tbsp (30 mL) grated
  Parmesan cheese

~~~~~~

1. Preheat the oven to 385°F (195°C).

2. Cook quinoa according to the instructions on the package, and set aside.

3. In a food processor, combine the onion, celery, carrots, and garlic, and pulse until finely blended.

4. Transfer to a frying pan and sauté in 2 Tbsp (30 mL) olive oil until the veggies soften. Salt and pepper to taste.

5. In a large bowl, mix together the quinoa, softened veggies, kale, ground turkey, horseradish, Dijon mustard, walnuts, egg, and the diced cornichon pickles. Mix well.

Continued on next page ↪

6. Put into a non-stick meatloaf pan and sprinkle with the Parmesan cheese.

7. Bake in the oven for 40 to 50 minutes until done.

8. Serve warm.

MAKES 4 TO 6 SERVINGS

NOTE: Serve with roast potatoes and a green salad, or cold the next day on gluten-free buns with lots of mayonnaise, lettuce, and tomato.

MEXICALI QUINOA

Hola! With the best avocado tree in the world in my backyard, I am an avocado freak. My daughter Lola loves them with fresh lime juice and scrambled eggs. This Mexican-inspired salad is so easy and tasty, it will soon become a staple in your gluten-free universe.

1 cup (250 mL) gluten-free
  corn tortillas, cut into strips
Vegetable oil (enough to cover
  the bottom of the pan by
  approx. 1 inch/2.5 cm)
2 cups (500 mL) red quinoa
½ cup (125 mL) finely diced
  red onion
2 cups (500 mL) diced avocado
1½ cups (375 mL) canned black
  beans, rinsed and drained

1 cup (250 mL) corn (canned,
  frozen or even grilled and
  taken off the cob)
¾ cup (185 mL) fresh cilantro,
  chopped + extra for garnish

DRESSING:

1 lime, juiced
1½ Tbsp (22.5 mL) honey
1 tsp (5 mL) Dijon mustard
¼ cup (60 mL) olive oil
Salt and pepper to taste

Why not try...adding some shredded chicken (see p.44) or grilled shrimp? Or roll the mixture up in rice wraps or corn tortillas and add some Monterey Jack cheese.

Or try grilling fresh corn for a smokier flavor. Same with the chicken. Just brush it with lemon, olive oil, salt and pepper, and barbecue. Cut it in cubes and you are good to go.

1. Fry the corn tortilla strips in vegetable oil until crisp. Set aside.

2. Cook the quinoa according to the instructions on the package and set aside.

3. In a large mixing bowl, combine quinoa, onion, avocado, black beans, corn, and fresh cilantro.

4. In a small bowl, whisk together lime juice, honey, mustard, and olive oil. Salt and pepper to taste.

5. Mix together the quinoa mixture and two-thirds of the dressing. Salt and pepper to taste. If you prefer a more heavily dressed quinoa, add the rest of the dressing.

6. Transfer to a platter and garnish with tortilla strips and more fresh cilantro.

MAKES APPROX. 6 CUPS (1.5 L)

MERRY CHRISTMAS QUINOA

I love mustard and bacon. It's almost my favorite combination, outside of cocktails and an ocean, or a great hair day when you have an important date. And by the way—you don't have to serve this only at Christmas.

½ cup (125 mL) diced onion

½ cup (125 mL) chopped pancetta or bacon

2 Tbsp (30 mL) olive oil

2 cups (500 mL) uncooked quinoa (why not try the red or black quinoa?)

1 cup (250 mL) diced celery

1 cup (250 mL) diced tart apples

1 cup (250 mL) pomegranate seeds

½ cup (125 mL) sultana raisins

½ cup (125 mL) walnuts

Salt and pepper to taste

DRESSING:

¼ cup (60 mL) olive oil

1 lemon, juiced

1 Tbsp (15 mL) gluten-free Worcestershire sauce

2 Tbsp (30 mL) grainy mustard

½ cup (125 mL) blue cheese, crumbled

½ cup (125 mL) chopped fresh Italian parsley

¼ cup (60 mL) dried cranberries for garnish

Amp it up!

To make it really festive, serve the quinoa in little radicchio cups as an appetizer.

1. In a sauté pan, fry the onions and pancetta (or bacon, if using) in the olive oil until cooked and a little crispy. Set aside.

2. Cook the quinoa according to the instructions on the package and set aside.

3. In a large mixing bowl, combine the quinoa, celery, apples, pomegranate seeds, raisins, and walnuts. Salt and pepper to taste.

4. In a small bowl, whisk together the olive oil, lemon juice, Worcestershire sauce, mustard, and blue cheese. The dressing will be chunky. Salt and pepper to taste.

5. Pour the dressing over the quinoa mixture and toss well. Add the bacon and onion mixture and the fresh Italian parsley and toss again.

6. Serve on a large platter and garnish with the dried cranberries.

MAKES APPROX. 6 CUPS (1.5 L)

LEMON ASPARAGUS RISOTTO

I love making risotto—the whole process. It is a bit time consuming but so worth the effort. Grab a glass of wine, crank up Prince on your iPod, and pretend you are on an Italian cruise (like I was last summer). Which, by the way, seems like ten years ago as I ask my son for maybe the twentieth time to take out the garbage. La dolce vita!

1 lb (450 g) asparagus stalks, divided
5 to 6 cups (1.25 to 1.5 L) gluten-free chicken stock
2 lemons, juiced
1 cup (250 mL) chopped shallots or sweet onions
¼ cup (60 mL) butter
1 Tbsp (15 mL) chopped fresh tarragon

Salt and pepper to taste
2 cups (500 mL) uncooked arborio rice
¼ cup (60 mL) white wine
1 cup (250 mL) grated Parmesan cheese + extra for garnish
¼ cup (60 mL) chopped fresh dill
Cracked black pepper

1. This is my little trick for delicious asparagus risotto. Take about 4 to 6 stalks of the asparagus and cook them—either blanch or microwave—until they're really soft. Purée in a food processor and add to your stock.

2. Blanch the rest of the asparagus until very al dente. When cool, cut into 1-inch (2.5 cm) pieces. Set aside.

3. Heat the stock with the puréed asparagus and lemon juice until warm, but not hot.

4. In a large pot, sauté the onions in butter until soft.

5. Add tarragon and salt and pepper. Then add the arborio rice, coat well with the butter mixture, and cook for about 2 to 3 minutes.

6. Deglaze the pot with the white wine and sauté for another 2 to 3 minutes.

7. Begin adding the warm stock ½ cup (125 mL) at a time, alternating with 1 to 2 Tbsp (15 to 30 mL) Parmesan cheese. Add a little salt and pepper.

8. Remember to constantly move the rice around. It needs lots of exercise while it absorbs the stock you're adding. Use a flat-ended wooden spoon and commit yourself to the procedure. Risotto demands your attention.

9. Keep adding the stock and Parmesan cheese until the rice is creamy and soft on the outside with a bit of bite in the center. The whole procedure usually takes 20 to 25 minutes. And don't freak out if you need more stock (or less) to get the perfect combination. It's a little different every time.

10. When the rice is almost done, add the blanched asparagus and mix well. Taste for seasoning and remove from heat.

11. Transfer to a large platter and finish with fresh dill, cracked black pepper, and more grated Parmesan cheese.

MAKES 4 TO 6 SERVINGS

PUMPKIN RISOTTO WITH CRISPY PANCETTA

This is a perfect winter or fall dish. Pull up a chair in front of the fireplace or throw a blanket down and have a picnic. Serve with a simple green salad with walnuts.

2 cups (500 mL) cubed pumpkin (cubes should be 1 inch/2.5 cm thick)
1 to 2 Tbsp (15 to 30 mL) olive oil
½ tsp (2.5 mL) salt + extra to taste
½ tsp (2.5 mL) pepper + extra to taste
2 Tbsp (30 mL) brown sugar + 1 Tbsp (15 mL) for baking the pumpkin (optional)
12 thin slices pancetta
5 to 6 cups (1.25 to 1.5 L) gluten-free chicken stock
1 cup (250 mL) chopped sweet onions
¼ cup (60 mL) butter

2 Tbsp (30 mL) chopped fresh rosemary + extra sprigs for garnish
2 Tbsp (30 mL) chopped fresh thyme
2 cups (500 mL) uncooked arborio rice
1 tsp (5 mL) ground nutmeg
½ tsp (2.5 mL) ground cloves
½ cup (125 mL) Calvados or Cointreau
1 cup (250 mL) grated Parmesan cheese + extra for garnish
1 Tbsp (15 mL) orange zest for garnish
Cracked black pepper for garnish

1. In a 385°F (195°C) oven, bake the cubed pumpkin in olive oil, salt, and pepper for approx. 25 to 35 minutes until cooked. You can add 1 Tbsp (15 mL) brown sugar if you want it slightly caramelized.

2. In a pan, fry the pancetta until crispy. Set aside.

3. Heat up the stock, making sure it is warm but not hot.

4. In a large pot, sauté the onions in butter until soft. Add the rosemary and thyme and sauté for another 1 to 2 minutes.

5. Add the cooked pumpkin and the arborio rice, and combine well with the onion and herb mixture.

6. Add the ground nutmeg, cloves, and 2 Tbsp (30 mL) brown sugar, and sauté for another 2 to 3 minutes.

7. Deglaze the pot with Calvados or Cointreau and allow to reduce for another 2 minutes.

8. Begin adding the stock ½ cup (125 mL) at a time, alternating with 1 to 2 Tbsp (15 to 30 mL) Parmesan cheese. Keep moving the rice around with a wooden spoon as the stock is absorbed. Repeat this procedure, seasoning as you go, until the rice is cooked through with a bit of a bite in the center, and the risotto has a creamy consistency. It usually takes between 20 and 25 minutes.

9. When the rice is done, mix in the crispy pancetta and transfer to a serving platter.

10. Garnish with the orange zest, lots of cracked black pepper, and freshly grated Parmesan, plus a few sprigs of rosemary.

MAKES 4 TO 6 SERVING

BROWN RICE PIE CRUST

Why not try...making a quiche? Whip up 4 eggs, 2 Tbsp (30 mL) half-and-half cream, ½ tsp (2.5 mL) ground nutmeg, 1 cup (250 mL) grated Swiss cheese, and ½ cup (125 mL) chopped Black Forest ham. Throw in some chopped thyme or Italian parsley or basil, pour mixture into the prebaked pie crust and bake at 375°F (190°C) for about 30 to 35 minutes until the egg is cooked through and a knife inserted in the center comes out clean. You can also sauté ½ cup (125 mL) shallots with ½ cup (125 mL) bacon instead of the ham.

This is such a simple recipe for pie crust using brown rice. You can fill it up any way you want—savory or sweet. I'll give you some suggestions.

1½ cups (375 mL) uncooked brown rice

½ cup (125 mL) grated Parmesan cheese

2 eggs, whisked

Salt and pepper to taste

1. Cook brown rice according to the instructions on the package and set aside.

2. Combine the rice, Parmesan cheese, eggs, and salt and pepper in a mixing bowl and blend well. Line a pie plate or baking pan with the mixture and bring the crust up 1 to 2 inches (2.5 to 5 cm) on the sides.

3. Bake in the oven at 385°F (195°C) for 20 to 25 minutes until golden brown.

4. Done!

MAKES 1 PIE CRUST

NOTE: Use some fresh thyme in the crust if you like.

Brown Rice Cheesecake

Make a savory cheesecake by mixing together a 15 oz (425 mL) can of puréed pumpkin, ¾ cup (185 mL) cream cheese, and 2 eggs. Add ½ cup (125 mL) diced red pepper, ¼ cup (60 mL) sundried tomatoes, ½ cup (125 mL) gluten-free breadcrumbs, ¼ cup (60 mL) chopped chives, and ½ cup (125 mL) grated Parmesan cheese. Mix well and set aside.

Prepare the brown rice crust (see previous page), covering only the bottom of a 9-inch (23 cm) springform pan (extra crust can be discarded). Bake the crust at 385° F (195° C) for 20 to 25 minutes until golden brown. Allow crust to cool and reduce oven temperature to 375°F (190°C). Pour cheesecake mixture onto the crust and bake for 25 to 30 minutes or until the pumpkin sets. Try using potatoes, or sweet potatoes, or parsnips. Be creative!

CONFETTI RICE

Why not try . . . serving it with grilled chicken or shrimp, marinated in olive oil, lemon juice, salt and pepper, and fresh herbs (basil, rosemary, thyme or whatever you have)?

Place a big pile of rice in the middle of the plate and artfully arrange sliced chicken or grilled shrimp around it.

Kids won't feel like they are missing anything with this delicious, action-packed rice dish. It's sweet, healthy, and vitamin rich. They might even want it for breakfast!

1 cup (250 mL) chopped green onions
1 Tbsp (15 mL) olive oil
1 Tbsp (15 mL) sesame oil
1 cup (250 mL) julienned red pepper
1½ cups (375 mL) uncooked basmati rice, brown or white
2½ cups (625 mL) gluten-free chicken stock
1 cup (250 mL) unsweetened coconut milk
½ cup (125 mL) fresh orange juice or apple juice
¼ cup (60 mL) organic peanut butter or almond butter
1 tsp (5 mL) ground turmeric
1 tsp (5 mL) ground cinnamon
Salt and pepper to taste
1 banana, chopped
½ cup (125 mL) peas, fresh or frozen
½ cup (125 mL) raisins
Chopped peanuts for garnish
Fresh cilantro for garnish

1. In a medium saucepan, sauté the green onions in the olive oil and sesame oil until soft.

2. Add the red pepper and cook for another 2 to 3 minutes.

3. Add the basmati rice and coat well with the onions and pepper.

4. Add the stock, coconut milk, orange juice (or apple juice) peanut butter (or almond butter), ground turmeric, cinnamon, and salt and pepper and bring to a boil. Reduce to medium-low heat and add the banana, peas, and raisins. Cook for 20 to 25 minutes until the rice is cooked and all the stock is absorbed. Garnish with chopped peanuts and fresh cilantro.

5. Yummy! And great for adults too.

MAKES 4 TO 6 SERVINGS

THE MOST DREADED WORDS IN THE ENGLISH LANGUAGE— WHAT'S FOR DINNER?

I have to say, nothing scares me more than having to come up with another way to make dinner delicious, fun, nutritious, blah blah blah! It's almost as bad as having to be creative about making lunches for your children for the entire school year. I felt it was really important for this book to give you the tools to make dinner hour not like an episode of *Breaking Bad*, but something that might actually verge on being enjoyable. What a concept!

RECIPES

BBQ PAELLA

This is my best friend Anne's favorite dish. She just made it for my birthday (29th), and it gets more delicious each time. The key to the dish is barbecuing the chorizo and chicken. But don't freak if you are snowed in—you can always use your indoor grill.

1½ lb (700 g) chicken thighs
   and breasts (skin-on, bone-in)
1 lb (450 g) chorizo sausage
2 Tbsp (30 mL) olive oil
Salt and pepper to taste
1 onion, chopped
1 red pepper, chopped
1 yellow pepper, chopped
2 tsp (10 mL) dried oregano

1 to 2 lemons, juiced
1½ cups (375 mL) uncooked
   arborio rice
4 cups (1 L) gluten-free
   chicken stock
1 cup (250 mL) frozen peas
1 cup (250 mL) chopped fresh
   Italian parsley
Lemon wedges for serving

Why not try . . . adding some saffron for a more authentic flavor? Just add a few saffron threads to your stock for color and flavor. You can also throw in 1 cup (250 mL) shrimp, if you like, at the end of the cooking process.

1. Brush the chicken and sausage with a little olive oil. Salt and pepper the chicken. Slightly char the chicken and the sausages on the BBQ or brown in a frying pan on medium-high heat and cook until about half done, about 8 to 10 minutes. (You can also roast the peppers if you want, but this is optional). Cut the sausage into medium-sized slices.

2. In a large pan, sauté the onion and peppers in the olive oil until they begin to soften. Add the dried oregano and lemon juice (adjust quantity to your taste), and cook for another 2 to 3 minutes.

3. Add the rice and mix well.

4. Add the chicken and sausage and cover with the rice mixture. Cook for another 3 minutes.

5. Add the stock and bring to a boil. Reduce to a simmer and cook until the rice is done, about 30 to 40 minutes. At the last minute, add the peas and cook for another 2 to 3 minutes.

6. Remove from the heat and stir in the parsley. Season with lots of salt and pepper.

7. Transfer to a large platter and serve with lemon wedges.

MAKES 4 TO 6 SERVINGS

HONEY MUSTARD SALMON WITH CANNELLINI BEANS

Amp it up!

You can use **Rosemary Roasted Potatoes** (see p. 119) instead of the cannellini beans. Or stir-fry the spinach and the beans in a little sesame oil and tamari sauce for more of an Asian flavor.

Why not try...coating

the salmon with 2 Tbsp (30 mL) honey? Salt and pepper and then pan fry.

NOTE: If you are really pressed for time, just sear the salmon without the marinade. Generously salt and pepper the salmon, and follow the cooking instructions. It's easy and still delicious.

This is a simple dish that packs a lot of flavor. I'm giving you a great marinade but, even if you just pan sear the salmon with a little olive oil and salt and pepper, the recipe works.

Four 6 to 8 oz (175 to 225 g) pieces of salmon
Salt and pepper to taste
½ cup (125 mL) gluten-free tamari sauce
3 Tbsp (45 mL) Dijon mustard
2 Tbsp (30 mL) brown sugar
1 Tbsp (15 mL) maple syrup
1 Tbsp (15 mL) chopped fresh ginger
1 Tbsp (15 mL) prepared horseradish
½ tsp (2.5 mL) lemon juice

2 Tbsp (30 mL) chopped fresh dill
1 to 2 Tbsp (15 to 30 mL) olive oil
4 cups (1 L) spinach
2 cups (500 mL) canned cannellini beans, drained
1 to 2 cups (250 to 500 mL) gluten-free chicken stock
1 Tbsp (15 mL) lemon zest for garnish
Cracked black pepper for garnish

1. Salt and pepper the salmon.

2. In a flat baking dish, mix together the tamari sauce, mustard, brown sugar, maple syrup, ginger, horseradish, lemon juice, and dill. Marinate the salmon for 1 to 2 hours, coating well with the mixture.

3. Remove the fish from the marinade and allow excess liquid to drain off.

4. Heat olive oil in a large sauté pan. Sear the salmon, skin side up, on medium-high heat for 3 to 4 minutes, or until the fish starts to get a nice golden, crispy texture. After 4 minutes, turn the fish over and cook for another 3 to 4 minutes, until it is firm to the touch. Some people like their salmon more pink while others prefer it cooked longer.

5. While the fish is cooking, heat up the spinach and the beans in the stock at a medium-high heat, about 5 to 8 minutes. Drain really well! Place on a plate or in large single serving bowls.

6. When the fish is cooked, place it on top of the spinach and bean mixture, angled slightly.

7. Garnish with lots of cracked black pepper and a little lemon zest.

MAKES 4 SERVINGS

HOISIN PORK WITH LETTUCE FOLDS

This is a great way to make Wednesday's dinner exotic and fun. When I was a little girl, we used to go out for Chinese food every Sunday and I would always order this dish—sweet, savory, and fresh all at the same time. This dish will soon become a family favorite.

Why not try...serving the pork on a gluten-free hamburger bun like a Sloppy Joe?

Or serving over greens with sliced avocado and jasmine rice?

2 Tbsp (30 mL) shredded fresh ginger

1 cup (250 mL) green onions, chopped

½ cup (125 mL) diced carrots

1 Tbsp (15 mL) peanut oil

1 lb (450 g) ground pork

⅓ cup (80 mL) homemade **Hoisin For Days** sauce (see p. 25)

½ cup (125 mL) gluten-free chicken stock

2 Tbsp (30 mL) gluten-free tamari sauce

1½ Tbsp (22.5 mL) maple syrup

¼ cup (60 mL) fresh basil, chopped

½ cup (125 mL) fresh cilantro, chopped

½ cup (125 mL) chopped salted peanuts for garnish

1 head iceberg lettuce

1. In a large frying pan, sauté the ginger, green onions, and carrots in the peanut oil for about 2 to 3 minutes.

2. Add the pork and cook for another 6 to 8 minutes, until almost done.

3. Add the **Hoisin For Days** sauce, the stock, tamari sauce, and maple syrup and mix well, cooking for another 6 to 8 minutes until the sauce starts to reduce and thicken.

4. Mix in the fresh basil and cilantro and transfer to a platter.

5. Garnish with the salted peanuts and serve with the cold, crisp lettuce leaves separated into little lettuce pockets that will be used to scoop up the pork.

MAKES 4 SERVINGS

OREGANO FETA MEATBALLS WITH ALMOND PILAF

Amp it up!

Make it really festive! Get some gluten-free wraps and make a meatball souvlaki. Serve with Lemon Feta Dip (see p. 32).

Everyone loves meatballs and this is a good basic recipe. They also go well with my **Italian Holiday Tomato Sauce** (see p. 19).

I cup (250 mL) gluten-free breadcrumbs
1 lb (450 g) lean ground beef
1 onion, grated
1 clove garlic, minced
2 Tbsp (30 mL) chopped fresh oregano, or dried
½ cup (125 mL) feta cheese

1 egg, beaten
Salt and pepper to taste
Almond Pilaf (recipe follows)
½ cup (125 mL) toasted almonds, sliced (see p. 24)
½ cup (125 mL) chopped fresh Italian parsley

1. To make the meatballs, mix together the breadcrumbs, ground beef, onion, garlic, oregano, feta cheese, and the egg. Mix well, and salt and pepper to taste.

2. Form into balls about 1½ inches (4 cm) in diameter and chill for about 1 hour.

3. Preheat your oven to 350°F (175°C).

4. Line a baking sheet with aluminum foil. Space the meatballs out on the baking sheet and cook for 15 to 20 minutes, until they start to brown. Turn once during the cooking time. Remove from the oven.

5. Serve the meatballs on a platter with the **Almond Pilaf** (recipe follows) and top with the toasted almond slices and Italian parsley.

MAKES 4 SERVINGS

ALMOND PILAF

2 Tbsp (30 mL) olive oil, divided
1½ cups (375 mL) uncooked
   jasmine or basmati rice
1 cup (250 mL) finely chopped
   onions

½ tsp (2.5 mL) ground turmeric
2 carrots, finely shredded
3 cups (750 mL) gluten-free
   chicken stock

1. Heat up 1 Tbsp (15 mL) olive oil in a pot over medium heat. Add the rice and move it around the pan, coating the rice with the oil until it starts to toast a little and becomes slightly golden, around 6 to 8 minutes. Transfer to a bowl and set aside.

2. In the same pot, sauté the onions in the remaining 1 Tbsp (15 mL) olive oil until they start to soften.

3. Coat the onions in the turmeric and add the carrots. Cook for 3 to 4 minutes.

4. Add the rice and coat well with the vegetable and turmeric mixture.

5. Add the stock and bring to a boil. Reduce heat to simmer and cook covered for 15 to 20 minutes, until the rice is done.

MAKES 3½ CUPS (875 ML)

GRILLED LAMB CHOPS WITH MINT PESTO

My friend Risa makes the best grilled lamb chops ever. I have amped it up a bit with some mint pesto and rosemary roasted potatoes.

12 lamb chops
Salt and pepper to taste
2 Tbsp (30 mL) olive oil
1 Tbsp (15 mL) Dijon mustard
2 Tbsp (30 mL) chopped fresh
   oregano

2 cloves garlic, minced
1 Tbsp (15 mL) lemon juice
Mint Pesto (recipe follows)
Rosemary Roasted Potatoes
   (recipe follows)

1. Salt and pepper the lamb chops.

2. In a large Ziploc bag, combine the olive oil, mustard, oregano, garlic, lemon juice, and a sprinkle of salt and pepper. Shake and mix well.

3. Put the lamb chops in the bag and marinate in the fridge for 2 to 3 hours.

4. Remove chops from the marinade and let the excess liquid drain off.

5. In a hot grill pan or on the barbecue, sear the lamb chops at medium-high heat, cooking for about 3 to 4 minutes on each side until desired doneness.

6. Serve the chops with a dollop of **Mint Pesto** and the **Rosemary Roasted Potatoes** (recipes follow).

MAKES 4 SERVINGS

NOTE: You can ask your butcher to leave the chops uncut and cook them in the **Mint Pesto** (recipe follows). Put the paste on the chops, all along the back, and bake in a 385°F (195°C) oven until done.

MINT PESTO

2 cups (500 mL) fresh mint
½ cup (125 mL) fresh basil
2 cloves garlic, minced
½ lemon, juiced
½ cup (125 mL) toasted pine
  nuts (see p. 24)

½ to ¾ cup (125 to 185 mL)
  grated Parmesan
¼ to ⅓ cup (60 to 80 mL)
  olive oil
Salt and pepper to taste

1. In a food processor, combine mint, basil, garlic, lemon juice, pine nuts, Parmesan cheese, and olive oil. Mix well and season with salt and pepper to taste. Adding more Parmesan cheese will make a chunkier paste.

MAKES 1½ CUPS (375 ML)

ROSEMARY ROASTED POTATOES

4 large potatoes, cut in wedges
4 parsnips, roughly chopped
½ lemon, juiced
3 to 4 Tbsp (45 to 60 mL)
  olive oil

2 Tbsp (30 mL) chopped fresh
  rosemary
Lots of salt and pepper

1. Preheat the oven to 400°F (200°C).

2. In a large bowl, mix together the potatoes, parsnips, olive oil, lemon juice, and fresh rosemary. Salt and pepper to taste.

3. Place mixture in a large roasting pan and cook for 55 to 65 minutes until veggies are golden brown.

MAKES 4 TO 6 SERVINGS

SESAME BEEF RICE BOWL

Why not try...using chicken instead of beef?

NOTE: Instead of steaming you can stir-fry the greens in a little soya sauce and sesame oil.

I just served this to 15 hungry people, some under four feet tall, and they lost their minds. I guarantee this will be my son Jack's favorite new dish.

2 cups (500 mL) uncooked sticky rice
1 lb (450 g) very thinly sliced beef, tender cut
1 Tbsp (15 mL) grated ginger
2 tsp (10 mL) minced garlic
½ Tbsp (7.5 mL) cornstarch
¼ cup (60 mL) gluten-free tamari sauce + extra for sautéing greens (optional)
2 Tbsp (30 mL) sugar
1 Tbsp (15 mL) rice vinegar
3 green onions, chopped

2 Tbsp (30 mL) sesame oil + extra for sautéing greens (optional)
½ lime, juiced
2 Tbsp (30 mL) toasted sesame seeds (see p. 24) + extra for sautéing greens
3 to 4 cups (750 mL to 1 L) Asian greens (bok choy, Chinese broccoli, collard greens, regular broccoli, rapini)
1 tsp (5 mL) freshly minced ginger (optional)

1. Cook the sticky rice according to the instructions on the package. Set aside.

2. In a medium-sized bowl, combine the thinly sliced beef, ginger, garlic, and the cornstarch, and mix well. Think of the cornstarch as a thickener, similar to dredging the meat through some flour when making a stew. Allow to marinate for about an hour in the fridge.

3. In a separate mixing bowl, combine the tamari sauce, sugar, rice vinegar, and green onions.

4. In a frying pan, add the sesame oil and stir-fry the beef for about 3 minutes, until it is almost cooked.

Continued on next page ᔆ

5.   Add the tamari mixture, bring to a boil, and reduce to a simmer as the sauce thickens.

6.   When almost done, finish with the lime juice and the toasted sesame seeds.

7.   For the Asian greens, either steam them or sauté in a large skillet over medium heat with 1 to 2 Tbsp (15 to 30 mL) sesame oil and gluten-free tamari sauce for flavor, depending on preference. You can also add 1 tsp (5 mL) freshly minced ginger and throw in 1 Tbsp (15 mL) sesame seeds.

8.   In separate bowls, serve the beef on a bed of sticky rice surrounded by Asian greens.

MAKES 4 SERVINGS

PISTACHIO CHICKEN ROLL UPS

The great thing about this recipe is that it is easy to make ahead of time, and it can be used in many ways. You can also get creative and make up fillings using leftovers or some of your favorite ingredients.

This is a popular dish with the under-12 crowd, who, by the way, can be the most difficult to cook for.

1 cup (250 mL) ricotta cheese
¼ cup (60 mL) pistachios, chopped
⅓ cup (80 mL) grated Parmesan cheese
2 Tbsp (30 mL) gluten-free breadcrumbs

¼ cup (60 mL) chopped fresh basil
¼ cup (60 mL) chopped sundried tomatoes
Salt and pepper to taste
4 skinless, boneless chicken breasts, pounded
Olive oil for frying

Amp it up!

There are lots of variations on this dish. You can use slices of eggplant or roasted red peppers for more depth. Also try rolling them up with some Black Forest ham and Swiss cheese. Use mascarpone or goat cheese with olives and capers for a different flavor. Be creative and experiment.

1. Mix together in a bowl, the ricotta cheese, pistachios, Parmesan cheese, breadcrumbs, fresh basil, and sundried tomatoes. Combine all ingredients well.

2. Salt and pepper the chicken breasts. Take about one-quarter of the filling and place it in the center of 1 of the chicken breasts and roll up. Tuck the sides under and wrap tightly in cling wrap. Repeat for the other 3 chicken breasts.

3. Chill the chicken for 1 to 2 hours before cooking—or overnight if you want.

4. Preheat the oven to 375°F (190°C).

5. In a sauté pan, heat the olive oil and brown the chicken roll ups on all sides.

6. Place the chicken roll ups in a non-stick baking dish and bake for 20 to 30 minutes until the chicken is cooked.

7. Remove from the oven and allow to cool for 10 minutes before slicing.

8. Slice the chicken on the bias and arrange on a large platter with either a green salad or a pile of jasmine rice in the middle. Colorful and delicious!

MAKES 4 SERVINGS

CRISPY SESAME CHICKEN WITH CURRIED COLESLAW

This recipe is a great combination of crispy fried chicken and fresh crunchy coleslaw. I had a version of this dish in Napa many years ago and fell in love with the flavorful combination.

1 cup (250 mL) rice flour
1 tsp (5 mL) Chinese five-spice powder
½ cup (125 mL) sesame seeds
½ Tbsp (7.5 mL) salt, divided + extra for seasoning
2 egg whites
4 skinless, boneless chicken breasts, cut into strips, approx. 2 inches (5 cm)
Peanut oil for frying

DRESSING:
2 Tbsp (30 mL) gluten-free curry paste (or use the **Curry Paste** recipe p. 49)

1 Tbsp (15 mL) Dijon mustard
2 Tbsp (30 mL) lime juice
2 Tbsp (30 mL) rice vinegar
1 tsp (5 mL) ground pepper + extra for seasoning
¼ cup (60 mL) olive oil

SALAD:
4 cups (1 L) Napa cabbage, purple and green, chopped
2 carrots, grated
¼ cup (60 mL) currants
¼ cup (60 mL) chopped fresh cilantro
Green onions for garnish
Salted peanuts for garnish

1. In a shallow baking dish, combine the rice flour, Chinese five-spice powder, sesame seeds, and 1 tsp (5 mL) of the salt.

2. In another shallow dish, whisk together the egg whites.

3. Dip the chicken slices in the egg white mixture and then dredge through the rice flour mixture.

4. Heat enough peanut oil in a pan to shallow-fry the chicken at medium-high heat.

5. Fry the chicken slices for about 2 to 3 minutes per side. Set aside. Keep warm in a 350°F (175°C) oven.

6. Meanwhile, in a small bowl whisk together the curry paste, mustard, lime juice, rice vinegar, ½ tsp (2.5 mL) salt, and 1 tsp (5 mL) pepper. When combined, slowly whisk in the olive oil until the dressing starts to thicken. Set aside.

7. In a large mixing bowl, combine the cabbage, grated carrots, and currants. Pour the curried dressing over the cabbage and toss in the cilantro. Salt and pepper to taste.

8. Serve the cabbage on a large platter with the crispy sesame chicken on top. Garnish with green onions and some salted peanuts. Or make individual plates for four.

MAKES 4 SERVINGS

ROASTED MUSTARD CHICKEN

Amp it up!

If you feel creative, you can always throw a whole head of garlic into the cavity of the bird, which gives it a sweet, smoky flavor. You can also throw some veggies into the pan for the last hour—potatoes, sweet potatoes, turnip, parsnip—whatever you like with your roast chicken.

If you know how to make a good roast chicken, you will go very far in life. It is a great classic dish that will always serve you well. Serve with a green salad, roasted veggies, or creamy mashed potatoes. Great for dinner, or for sandwiches or soup the next day. It's a must for any occasion. This version comes from my friend Anne, whom I have known since Grade 8 and who is still as crazy and immature as she was when I met her at the mall. How great is that? She forced me to use thyme instead of rosemary—beeyatch!

3 Tbsp (45 mL) Dijon mustard
2 shallots
2 cloves garlic
Salt and pepper to taste
One 8 to 9 lb (3.5 to 4 kg)
  capon or chicken
2 lemons, quartered

½ cup (125 mL) fresh thyme,
  chopped
2 onions, quartered
Olive oil (enough to coat the
  chicken)
Kosher salt and cracked black
  pepper for seasoning

1. Preheat the oven to 400°F (200°C).

2. In a food processor combine the mustard, shallots, garlic and salt and pepper to taste. Pulse into a rough paste.

3. Peel back the skin from the chicken and rub the mustard sauce between the skin and the flesh. Do it all over the bird. I know it's messy, but it is so worth it.

4. Stuff the cavity with the lemons and the fresh thyme. Bend the wings back so they tuck under, and tie the legs together crisscrossed to keep the cavity closed.

5. Place in a large roasting pan (see note) on top of the quartered onions. Cover the bird well with olive oil, kosher salt, and cracked black pepper. Roast for 20 minutes at 400°F (200°C) then turn the oven down to 375°F (190°C) for the remainder of the cooking time, about 2 ½ to 3 hours. I use 20 minutes per pound as a standard, but you can use an internal thermometer—the thigh should read 170 to 180°F (77 to 82°C)—or you can puncture the skin around the thigh with a knife to check for clear juices. Baste every 20 minutes.

6. When done, allow to sit for 10 to 15 minutes before carving and serving.

MAKES 6 SERVINGS

NOTE: You can cover the bottom of the pan with 1 chopped onion and some roughly chopped carrots and parsnips for added flavor.

SPINACH POTATO TORTILLA

This is a quick version of the Spanish tortilla that is frequently served for tapas—with lots of sangria! It's great hot, or served cold the next day with polenta or a green salad.

2 to 3 medium potatoes, skinned
Salt to taste
3 to 4 Tbsp (45 to 60 mL) olive oil
3 cups (750 mL) thinly sliced onions

1 Tbsp (15 mL) chopped fresh thyme, or dried thyme
½ lemon, juiced
Cracked black pepper to taste
6 eggs, lightly beaten and seasoned

1. Cook the potatoes in a large pot of boiling water until half done with a good bite to them, about 8 to 10 minutes. Allow them to cool, then thinly slice and salt.

2. Preheat the broiler to medium, or the oven to 500°F (260°C).

3. Heat the oil over a medium heat in a medium-sized skillet with a heatproof handle.

4. Add the onion and sauté until golden and soft, about 10 minutes.

5. Add the thyme and cook for another 1 to 2 minutes.

6. Add the potatoes and lemon juice and cook for another 5 to 6 minutes, stirring to prevent the potatoes from sticking. They should be cooked with a little bite in the center.

7. Spread the onions and potatoes evenly over the bottom of the skillet and season well with salt and pepper.

8. Pour the egg mixture over the potatoes and cook for another 5 to 6 minutes until the eggs set and the potatoes start to golden.

9. Put the skillet under the broiler and cook for 2 to 4 minutes until the eggs begin to rise and cook on top.

10. Allow to cool slightly and then cut into wedges.

MAKES 4 TO 6 SERVINGS

NOTE: Serve with a green salad full of walnuts and arugula. Have little dishes of olives and smoked almonds, and jugs of sangria—who cares if it's a weekday!

CHICKPEA STEW WITH FETA AND HONEY

This is one of my most requested vegetable dishes. It is fresh and tangy and substantial, all at the same time. This dish has lots of extra sauce for dipping and soaking up with rice or gluten-free pita or bread! Great for a dinner party where everyone can dig in family style, or alone in your room on a rainy night, imagining yourself in Tangiers, shopping for rugs and exotic fabric . . .

NOTE: Serve with basmati rice and some mango or lime chutney.

1 tsp (5 mL) tomato paste
One 28 oz (796 g) can crushed
    tomatoes
2 Tbsp (30 mL) gluten-free
    curry paste (or use the **Curry
    Paste** recipe p. 49)
1 tsp (5 mL) ground cumin
1 tsp (5 mL) ground turmeric
1 clove garlic
2 Tbsp (30 mL) honey
1 Tbsp (15 mL) brown sugar
1 cup (250 mL) plain Greek
    yogurt

½ cup (125 mL) fresh cilantro
    + extra for garnish
1 lime, juiced
1 tsp (5 mL) fresh ginger
½ cup (125 mL) diced sweet
    onions
2 Tbsp (30 mL) olive oil
3 cups (750 mL) canned
    chickpeas, drained and rinsed
4 cups (1 L) fresh spinach
2 cups (500 mL) cubed feta
    cheese
Cracked black pepper to taste

1. In a food processor, combine the tomato paste, crushed tomatoes, curry paste, ground cumin, ground turmeric, garlic, honey, brown sugar, Greek yogurt, cilantro, lime juice, and fresh ginger. Blend well.

2. In a large pan, sauté the onions in olive oil until they are soft.

3. Add the processed sauce and the chickpeas and cook for about 5 to 7 minutes until the sauce begins to thicken. Add the spinach and cook until wilted.

4. Add the feta cheese at the last minute, warming it up but not to the point that it melts—you want it in cubes.

5. Transfer to a colorful bowl or platter and garnish with more fresh cilantro and cracked black pepper.

MAKES 4 SERVINGS

BLACK BEAN FRITTERS WITH MANGO SALSA

Why not try...a simple dinner, by whipping up some guacamole and serving the fritters with corn tortillas and Mexican rice? For the rice, take 1 cup (250 mL) onions, 1½ cups (375 mL) rice to 3 cups (750 mL) stock and 1 Tbsp (15 mL) tomato paste. Add ½ cup (125 mL) chopped cilantro and a little lime juice when the rice is cooked, and you are ready to go.

Or make black bean fritter stacks. Place a couple of slices of avocado and a dollop of salsa on top of the fritter. You can double the protein by topping the fritters with shredded chicken (see p. 44) and avocado.

This is a great healthy dinner packed with protein. It is now officially Lola's favorite recipe.

1 cup (250 mL) gluten-free flour
½ Tbsp (7.5 mL) gluten-free baking powder
½ tsp (2.5 mL) salt
1 egg, beaten
¾ cup (185 mL) coconut milk or almond milk
2½ cups (625 mL) thinly sliced scallions

2 cups (500 mL) canned black beans, drained
½ cup (125 mL) chopped fresh cilantro + extra for garnish
Salt and pepper to taste
Canola oil for frying (enough to cover the bottom of the skillet by approx. ½ to ¾ inch/1 to 2 cm)

1. In a large mixing bowl, sift the flour, baking powder, and salt. Make a hole in the center and add the egg and the milk. Stir into the flour, making a smooth batter.

2. Mix in the scallions, black beans, and fresh cilantro. Season well with salt and pepper.

3. Heat up the oil in a large heavy skillet and add 1 Tbsp (15 mL) heaps of the mixture for each fritter. Cook about 4 to 6 fritters at a time, for about 4 to 6 minutes until golden brown, turning once.

4. Serve fritters with **Mango Salsa** (recipe follows) on a large platter and garnish with fresh cilantro.

MAKES 4 SERVINGS

MANGO SALSA

1 mango, chopped
¼ red pepper, diced
⅓ cup (80 mL) diced red onion

¼ cup (60 mL) chopped fresh
  cilantro
1 Tbsp (15 mL) lime juice
Salt and pepper to taste

1. Mix together mango, red pepper, red onion, cilantro, and lime juice, and
    season well with salt and pepper.

MAKES ¾ TO 1 CUP (185 TO 250 ML)

SNACKS AND LAST MINUTE KNOSHES

Those damn snacks—they can bring all of us down
so fast! It's a good idea to preplan them or make
sure they are really easy to make so you don't get
sucked into the crappy snack vortex. Some can be
made up in big batches and others work last minute.

RECIPES

LENTIL PURÉE AND QUINOA RICE WRAPS

This is a good basic lentil purée that you can use in sandwiches, or as a dip for chicken or veggies. You can also tart it up by adding sundried tomatoes, olives, capers, cornichons, or whatever you like, for a burst of flavor.

2½ cups (625 mL) cooked red lentils (see p. 29)
¼ cup (60 mL) olive oil
1 lemon, juiced
1 clove garlic
1 Tbsp (15 mL) Dijon mustard
½ tsp (2.5 mL) prepared horseradish
1 tsp (5 mL) paprika
½ tsp (2.5 mL) ground turmeric

Kosher salt and cracked black pepper to taste
½ cup (125 mL) uncooked quinoa
4 rice wraps
1 avocado, sliced
¼ cup (60 mL) chopped fresh cilantro + extra for garnish
1 to 2 cups (250 to 500 mL) chopped kale or romaine
1 tomato, diced

Amp it up!

Throw other things into the wraps—black beans, grilled eggplant, roasted peppers, some of our chicken salad (see p. 138)—whatever appeals to you. The lentils are a great source of protein.

1. Put the lentils, olive oil, lemon juice, garlic, mustard, horseradish, paprika, and turmeric into a food processor. Blend until smooth and then season with kosher salt and cracked black pepper.

2. Cook the quinoa according to the instructions on the package and set aside.

3. Line each wrap with the lentil purée, then a scoop of quinoa, some avocado, chopped cilantro, chopped kale (or romaine), and some diced tomato. Garnish with a little more fresh cilantro and roll up.

MAKES 4 WRAPS

NOTE: Recipe makes approx. 2½ cups (625 mL) lentil purée. Extra purée is great as a dip for veggies or chicken.

CHICKEN SALAD WRAPS

Why not try...

serving it on a bed of arugula
and mandarin oranges?

Chicken salad is one of my favorite things. I love it with greens, on a sandwich, or served in little iceberg lettuce pockets for a real burst of freshness. It's a good idea to make a big batch to have on-hand for last-minute healthy treats and lunches.

2 cups (500 mL) shredded or cubed cooked chicken (see p. 44)

1 cup (250 mL) diced green apples

½ cup (125 mL) green grapes, cut in half

½ cup (125 mL) chopped walnuts

¼ cup (60 mL) mayonnaise

2 Tbsp (30 mL) Greek yogurt

¼ cup (60 mL) dried cranberries

Salt and pepper to taste

6 to 8 iceberg lettuce leaves

1. In a large bowl, mix together the chicken, green apples, grapes, walnuts, mayonnaise, yogurt, and cranberries. Mix well and salt and pepper to taste.

2. Wrap the chicken salad in the iceberg lettuce leaves. They're like perfect little jewels!

MAKES 4 SERVINGS

CURRIED TUNA POCKETS

This is a great quick snack for kids and gives them a good boost of protein. Serve in a gluten-free wrap, or on top of a gluten-free bagel. You can also serve it in lettuce pockets or in celery sticks.

Three 5 oz (142 g) cans albacore tuna
½ cup (125 mL) chopped celery
½ cup (125 mL) chopped green onions
1 cup (250 mL) fresh or canned (drained) pineapple, chopped
¼ cup (60 mL) dried organic apricots, chopped

DRESSING:
¼ cup (60 mL) Greek yogurt
¼ cup (60 mL) mayonnaise
½ cup (125 mL) chopped fresh cilantro
1 Tbsp (15 mL) gluten-free curry paste (or use the **Curry Paste** recipe p. 49)
½ lime, juiced

Salt and pepper to taste
½ cup (125 mL) pistachios
Shredded coconut for garnish

Why not try . . . using crab or shredded chicken (see p. 44)—or even lobster—instead of tuna? Throw in a banana or mango instead of the pineapple. Cashews would work too.

1. Drain the tuna very well.

2. In a large bowl, combine the tuna, celery, green onions, pineapple, and apricots. Mix well.

3. In a small bowl, combine the yogurt, mayonnaise, cilantro, curry paste, and lime juice. Mix together with the tuna mixture.

4. Mix again, adding salt and pepper and the pistachios.

5. Garnish with shredded coconut.

MAKES 4 TO 6 SERVINGS

JACK'S DEVILED EGGS

VARIATIONS

❦   ❦

Keep the same basic mixture, minus the relish and add these ingredients. You can also add a bit of the relish at the end if you want a little kick! Be creative and have fun!

KENTUCKY DERBY EGGS
Add 2 Tbsp (30 mL) chopped watercress with 2 Tbsp (30 mL) chopped bacon.

PARISIAN AFTERNOON
Use 2 Tbsp (30 mL) chopped cornichons with 1 Tbsp (15 mL) chopped fresh dill.

STROMBOLI SUNSET
Add 2 Tbsp (30 mL) chopped sundried tomatoes or olives with 1 Tbsp (15 mL) chopped fresh basil.

BAJA EGGS
Add 2 Tbsp (30 mL) mashed avocado, 1 Tbsp (15 mL) salsa, and 1 Tbsp (15 mL) chopped fresh cilantro.

EAST COAST MORNING
Add about 2 Tbsp (30 mL) chopped smoked salmon with 1 tsp (5 mL) finely diced red onion and 1 tsp (5 mL) capers.

Jack and I are crazy about deviled eggs. The best I have ever had come from my great friend Chris, who served them on his finest china with doilies, and also some I had in Lexington, Kentucky, at a literary festival. This is a basic recipe with variations.

12 whole fresh eggs, boiled and peeled (see sidebar)
1½ tsp (7.5 mL) good pickled relish
½ tsp (2.5 mL) Dijon mustard
¼ tsp (1 mL) onion powder
¼ tsp (1 mL) cayenne pepper
½ cup (125 mL) mayonnaise
⅓ cup (80 mL) sour cream
Paprika to taste
¼ cup (60 mL) chopped fresh chives

1. Cut the peeled eggs in half, lengthwise.

2. Carefully scoop out the egg yolks and, in a small bowl, combine with the relish, mustard, onion powder, cayenne pepper, mayonnaise, and sour cream. Mix well.

3. Set the egg white halves on a sturdy surface—you might even want to trim a bit off the bottom of the eggs to keep them flat.

4. Put the yolk mixture into a piping bag and fill the egg white halves. You can also use a plastic bag—the freezer Ziploc bags work well. Just cut a small hole in the corner to mimic a piping bag.

5. Garnish with the paprika and chives.

MAKES 24 DEVILED EGGS

To Boil the Perfect Egg:

I have done lots of research on this and boiled many eggs. In a large pot, cover the eggs by an extra 1 inch (2.5 cm) with cold water. Add 1 Tbsp (15 mL) white vinegar and about 1 Tbsp (15 mL) salt—the vinegar prevents the egg white from running out of the eggs while cooking, and the salt keeps the eggs from cracking and makes them easier to peel. Bring the water to a boil and cook for about 1 minute. Remove the pot from heat and cover with a lid. Let stand for about 12 minutes.

After 12 minutes, remove the eggs with a slotted spoon and put them in a bowl of ice water for a few minutes, until cool enough to peel.

POLENTA BRUSCHETTA

Why not try...cutting the polenta into circles and stacking them? Use eggplant, red peppers, zucchini, or whatever you like, alternating with goat cheese or **Citrus Hummus** (see p. 67). Add some prosciutto, with avocado and cantaloupe shavings.

Polenta is corn based so it is gluten-free. This is a basic recipe that you can use as a base for lots of things. Here we are using it for bruschetta with a tomato mixture on top, but you could also use it as a base for a sandwich, or cut it into circles for appetizers or layering. It will become a new staple.

TOMATO MIXTURE:
½ cup (125 mL) finely diced onions
2 tsp (10 mL) **Roasted Garlic Paste** (see p. 33) or 2 cloves garlic, minced
2½ cups (625 mL) diced tomatoes
2 Tbsp (30 mL) balsamic vinegar
¼ cup (60 mL) olive oil
1 tsp (5 mL) anchovy paste
1 tsp (5 mL) Dijon mustard
½ cup (125 mL) chopped fresh basil + extra for garnish
¼ cup (60 mL) grated Parmesan cheese
1 Tbsp (15 mL) lemon juice

POLENTA:
7 to 8 cups (1.75 to 2 L) gluten-free chicken stock
1 tsp (5 mL) sea salt + extra for seasoning
1 cup (250 mL) cornmeal
2 Tbsp (30 mL) chopped fresh thyme
Olive oil for brushing
½ cup (125 mL) crumbled goat cheese
Cracked black pepper to taste

1. Mix together the onions, garlic, diced tomatoes, vinegar, olive oil, anchovy paste, mustard, basil, Parmesan cheese, and lemon juice. Set aside and let marinade while you make the polenta.

2. Bring the stock and 1 tsp (5 mL) salt to a boil, then reduce to medium heat. Add the cornmeal slowly, whisking it in until the stock is completely absorbed.

3. Reduce to low heat, stirring occasionally so it does not stick.

4. The polenta is cooked when it has the consistency of mashed potatoes and falls away from the pan—it is quite dense and thick. This usually takes about 35 to 40 minutes. When almost done, stir in the thyme and the salt and pepper to season.

5. Spread the polenta onto a baking sheet to a thickness of about ¾ inch (2 cm). Allow to cool and then cut into desired shape—about 8 to 10 pieces for the bruschetta. Brush with olive oil and bake under the broiler on medium until golden brown, turning once, or fry in a pan.

6. When the polenta is done, remove from the oven or frying pan and place on a platter. Use a slotted spoon when putting the tomato mixture on top of the polenta to drain a lot of the excess liquid. Sprinkle with the goat cheese and serve.

7. Garnish with cracked black pepper and more fresh basil.

MAKES 4 TO 6 SERVINGS

ZUCCHINI TORTILLAS

I had this the other night at a restaurant and it was the freshest appetizer I've had in a while. Simple, with great basic ingredients, it was a fantastic way to kick off a four-hour reunion dinner with one of my best friends. As a matter of fact, we managed to eat two full orders.

3 medium zucchinis (see note)
3 Tbsp (45 mL) olive oil
½ lemon, juiced
1 tsp (5 mL) chopped fresh
    thyme or lemon thyme
Salt and pepper to taste

12 small corn tortillas
1 cup (250 mL) crumbled
    creamy goat cheese
¼ cup (60 mL) honey
¾ cup (185 mL) walnuts
12 fresh mint leaves

NOTE: You can grill the zucchini or serve fresh, whichever you prefer. If grilling, slice zucchini thicker so it holds up on the grill. Heat oven to 385°F (195°C) and cook zucchini in a grill pan or on a baking sheet for about 18 to 20 minutes, until it starts to golden. Salt and pepper to taste.

1. Slice the zucchini very thin. Place in a bowl with olive oil, lemon juice, fresh thyme, and salt and pepper to taste.

2. To serve, line each tortilla with a couple of slices of zucchini.

3. Top with some goat cheese, a drizzle of honey, and some walnuts.

4. Add a mint leaf to each one and leave open for your guests to roll up.

5. Sublime!

MAKES 4 SERVINGS

COCONUT SESAME BEANS

Kids love these beans. Crunchy, sweet, and salty, they add an exotic flare to any meal. They're also great as a full-course meal—just add grilled shrimp or stir-fried beef tenderloin.

DRESSING:
¾ cup (185 mL) coconut milk
1 lime, juiced
2½ Tbsp (37.5 mL) crunchy
    peanut butter
1 Tbsp (15 mL) chopped fresh
    ginger
1 Tbsp (15 mL) brown sugar
1 Tbsp (15 mL) fish sauce

1 cup (250 mL) sliced shallots
2 Tbsp (30 mL) butter
Salt and pepper for seasoning
5 cups (1.25 L) fresh green
    beans, trimmed and blanched
½ cup (125 mL) toasted sesame
    seeds (see p. 24)
¼ cup (60 mL) chopped fresh
    cilantro
¼ cup (60 mL) chopped
    fresh mint
¼ cup (60 mL) chopped fresh
    basil, for garnish
¼ cup (60 mL) crushed peanuts,
    for garnish
Cracked black pepper

1. In a bowl, whisk together the coconut milk, lime juice, peanut butter, ginger, brown sugar, and the fish sauce. Mix well.

2. In a medium pan, sauté the shallots in the butter until soft. Season with salt and pepper.

3. In a large bowl mix the shallots, green beans, sesame seeds, cilantro, and mint. Add the dressing and toss well.

4. Transfer to a large platter or bowl. Garnish with the fresh basil and peanuts and lots of cracked black pepper.

MAKES 4 SERVINGS

ICEBERG WEDGE TREAT

I love Cobb salad and this is a simple variation on that theme. Delicious and easy to whip up, it works as a snack, a quick lunch, or an appetizer for a dinner party. It also looks great on a plate.

Why not try...cutting the iceberg in wedges and pouring the salad mixture on top!

1 cup (250 mL) green beans, julienned
1 head of iceberg lettuce
3 to 4 strips uncooked bacon
4 hard-boiled eggs, chopped
¼ cup (60 mL) chopped walnuts

DRESSING:
¼ cup (60 mL) olive oil
¼ cup (60 mL) balsamic or red wine vinegar

2 Tbsp (30 mL) Dijon mustard
2 Tbsp (30 mL) chopped fresh basil
Salt and pepper to taste

½ cup (125 mL) crumbled blue cheese for garnish
Grated Parmesan cheese for garnish
Cracked black pepper

1. Bring green beans to a boil in a pot of water, then reduce heat to medium-low and simmer until beans start to soften, approx. 5 minutes. Drain and set aside.

2. Take a head of iceberg lettuce and cut it in half lengthwise so you have two sections of lettuce cups.

3. In a non-stick frying pan, cook bacon over medium heat until crispy. Allow to cool, then chop and set aside.

4. In a medium-sized bowl, combine the bacon, eggs, walnuts, and the julienned green beans.

5. In a small bowl, whisk together the olive oil, vinegar, mustard, and chopped fresh basil. Salt and pepper to season.

6. Divide the egg and bacon mixture evenly among the lettuce cups, garnishing each one with the blue cheese.

7. Drizzle each one with the dressing and lots of freshly grated Parmesan and cracked black pepper.

MAKES 4 SERVINGS

POTATO PANCAKE BREAKFAST SANDWICHES

Why not try...making a classic BLT? Use the potato pancakes as a base and build a sandwich using sliced tomatoes, bacon, lettuce, and mayonnaise.

This is a great weekend breakfast to really get your day going. The potato pancakes are easy to make and you can be creative with the filling. I use potatoes in this recipe, but carrots, celeriac, or sweet potatoes would also be good.

2 large potatoes, shredded, or 2 cups (500 mL) shredded celeriac, carrots, or sweet potatoes

Salt and pepper to taste

¼ cup (60 mL) butter, divided (melt 2 Tbsp/30 mL, leave the rest solid)

2 Tbsp (30 mL) gluten-free flour

2 Tbsp (30 mL) chopped fresh Italian parsley, chives, or dill

2 to 4 Tbsp (30 to 60 mL) canola or sunflower oil (add more as needed)

4 eggs

1 Tbsp (15 mL) whipping cream

1 green onion, chopped

2 Tbsp (30 mL) chopped fresh Italian parsley

½ cup (125 mL) grated Parmesan cheese

1 avocado, sliced

I cup (250 mL) crème fraîche

Fresh parsley for garnish

1. Preheat the oven to 350°F (175°C).

2. Place the shredded potatoes into a bowl. Salt and pepper to taste. Add the melted butter, flour, chopped parsley (or chives, or dill), and mix well.

3. Cover the bottom of a heavy frying pan with the canola or sunflower oil. Pour in enough of the potato batter to make a 3-inch (8 cm) round pancake, about ¼ cup (60 mL). Pat the pancake down flat and fry in the oil until golden brown. Repeat as needed; you should get 8 pancakes. Put them in a baking dish in the oven to keep warm.

Continued on next page ↬

4. In a medium-sized bowl, mix together the eggs, cream, green onion, parsley, and salt and pepper to taste.

5. Heat a skillet to medium and melt the remaining 2 Tbsp (30 mL) butter. Pour the egg mixture into the pan, constantly moving it around until the eggs begin to scramble and cook, around 4 to 5 minutes. Top with Parmesan cheese.

6. To assemble the sandwiches, place some scrambled eggs on a potato pancake, then top with avocado slices. Put another pancake on top with a dollop of crème fraîche and chopped fresh parsley.

MAKES 4 SERVINGS

FRUIT PARFAIT WITH HONEY GRANOLA

This is good as a snack or for breakfast! Use some Mason jars and layer the fruit, granola, and yogurt in them. I have doubled the amount of granola so there will be extra.

3 cups (750 mL) rice flakes or buckwheat flakes

5 Tbsp (75 mL) honey, divided

2 Tbsp (30 mL) crushed pistachios

½ cup (125 mL) raisins, dates or currants (optional)

3 cups (750 mL) Greek yogurt

2 cups (500 mL) fresh berries or frozen, any kind + extra for garnish

2 tsp (10 mL) grated orange rind

Fresh mint leaves for garnish

Why not try ... using pineapple, mango, banana, or whatever fruit you like?

1. In a dry skillet over medium heat, add the flakes and toast for about 1 to 2 minutes, shaking them around in the pan. Add 4 Tbsp (60 mL) honey and the pistachios, coating the flakes and stirring constantly, until golden brown and a little crispy. Add in raisins, dates, or currants, if using.

2. In a bowl, stir together the yogurt, berries, the rest of the honey, and the orange rind. Save a few berries for garnish.

3. Let sit for about 5 to 10 minutes, then layer with the granola in the Mason jars—granola first, yogurt mixture, granola, yogurt mixture. Garnish with the mint leaves.

MAKES 4 SERVINGS

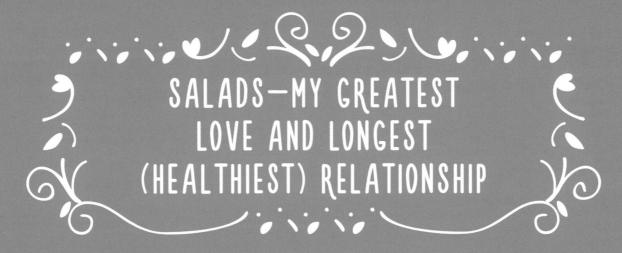

SALADS—MY GREATEST LOVE AND LONGEST (HEALTHIEST) RELATIONSHIP

Ever since I can remember, I have had a love affair with salads. Even as a kid, I was always first in line for the salad bar. From the hard-boiled eggs to the weird green aspic, I was in! And as I grew older, I became known for my uncanny ability to combine lettuce with almost anything. Imagine my delight when arugula, warm salads, and salads with bacon and nuts came into my lexicon. I was hooked! I have also found that kids will eat heaps of greens with one simple caveat: It just has to taste good. What a concept . . .

RECIPES

WARM CHICKEN SALAD WITH HONEY MUSTARD DRESSING

This is a substantial salad that is great with dinner or on its own. The warm rice and crisp romaine lettuce make it the perfect way to satisfy all customers.

¾ cup (185 mL) uncooked rice

2 chicken breasts, skinless, boneless

3 cups (750 mL) chopped romaine lettuce

1 cup (250 mL) diced tomatoes

½ cup (125 mL) sliced red onions

¼ cup (60 mL) honey

5 Tbsp (75 mL) Dijon mustard

¼ cup (60 mL) rice wine vinegar or apple cider vinegar

½ cup (125 mL) crumbled feta cheese

¼ cup (60 mL) chopped Italian parsley

Cracked black pepper

1. Cook rice according to the instructions on the package. Set aside.

2. Preheat your oven to 375°F (190°C) and bake chicken for 30 to 35 minutes, until done. Remove and set aside until cool enough to handle, then cut into cubes.

3. In a large bowl or on a platter, place the romaine lettuce first, then the tomatoes and the red onions. Layer the chicken next.

4. In a small bowl whisk together the honey, mustard, and vinegar. Set aside.

5. Right before serving, put the warm rice on top of the chicken, then the feta cheese, and pour most of the honey mustard dressing over everything. Toss well and taste to see if you need more dressing.

6. Serve in separate bowls with lots of cracked black pepper and a little freshly chopped Italian parsley.

MAKES 4 TO 6 SERVINGS

NOTE: I like a lot of dressing, but you might want to start with three-quarters of the dressing and add on from there.

VENTURA BLVD CHOPPED SALAD

some thinly sliced beef
tenderloin, stir-fried in
sesame oil? Toss
it with toasted sesame seeds
for an extra punch.

Or make it totally vegetarian. Take
out the chicken and add some red
and yellow beets.
Or try sweet potatoes.

NOTE: Feel free to replace
the olive oil and vinger with
the **Citrus Mash** salad dressing
(see p. 17).

This has quickly become one of my favorite salads for two rea-sons—it is crazy simple to make and has at least three of my favorite things in it. I love this salad with a glass of crisp white wine and great company. You just chop everything up and it becomes a pile of deliciousness.

2 chicken breasts, skinless, boneless
5 to 6 Tbsp (75 to 90 mL) olive oil, divided
1 Tbsp (15 mL) lemon juice
Salt and pepper to taste
1 tsp (5 mL) chopped fresh thyme or rosemary (optional)
6 strips of bacon
4 cups (1 L) chopped romaine lettuce
1 cup (250 mL) hearts of palm, cut on the bias

½ cup (125 mL) diced tomatoes
1 avocado, diced
1 cup (250 mL) crumbled feta cheese
½ cup (125 mL) shelled pistachios, chopped
¼ cup (60 mL) chopped fresh basil
2 Tbsp (30 mL) balsamic vinegar
Cracked black pepper

1. Preheat your oven to 375°F (190°C). Toss the chicken in 1 to 2 Tbsp (15 to 30 mL) olive oil, the lemon juice, and salt and pepper. Place the chicken on a baking pan and into the oven for 30 to 35 minutes, until done. Remove and set aside to cool, then cut into cubes. You can also amp the flavor by adding 1 tsp (5 mL) chopped fresh thyme or rosemary!

2. In a non-stick frying pan, cook the bacon over medium heat until crispy. Allow to cool, then chop and set aside.

3. Place the choped romaine in a large bowl. Add the diced chicken, bacon, hearts of palm, tomatoes, and avocado. The goal is to have everything chopped to roughly the same size. Add the feta, the pistachios, and the fresh basil. Toss well and lightly dress, drizzling with the remaining 4 to 5 Tbsp (60 to 75 mL) olive oil and the balsamic vinegar. Add lots of salt and cracked black pepper.

MAKES 4 SERVINGS

SHREDDED BASIL CHICKEN WITH MANGO

This is a simple salad that will make you think you are on vacation somewhere really exotic. Make yourself a cocktail, plug in your MP3 player, and ignore everyone—the perfect recipe for a stress-free afternoon!

Why not try...skipping the noodles and serving it on a bed of greens or with rice?

5 oz (140 g) dried thin rice noodles

¼ cup (60 mL) toasted sesame seeds (see p. 24)

5 cups (1.25 L) shredded chicken (see p. 44)

1 cup (250 mL) shredded fresh basil

1 mango, unripe, julienned

3 Tbsp (45 mL) fish sauce

3 Tbsp (45 mL) lime juice

2 Tbsp (30 mL) brown sugar

1 tsp (5 mL) chopped fresh chili pepper, seeded

½ cup (125 mL) shredded fresh mint

1 cup (250 mL) bean sprouts

Cracked black pepper to taste

1. Cook the rice noodles following the instructions on the package, being careful not to overcook them. If you do, run them under cold water and separate.

2. In a large bowl, combine the noodles, toasted sesame seeds, shredded chicken, basil, and julienned mango.

3. In a small bowl, whisk together the fish sauce, lime juice, brown sugar, and the chopped fresh chili.

4. Pour the dressing over the chicken mixture and toss well. Add the mint and toss again.

5. Serve on a large platter or in a big colorful bowl and garnish with the bean sprouts and lots of cracked black pepper.

MAKES 4 TO 6 SERVINGS

THAI PORK AND RICE SALAD

This is a very fresh salad and adding pork makes it a bit more substantial. I have also added crispy, cold iceberg lettuce and basmati rice to make it even more delicious.

1 cup (250 mL) uncooked basmati rice

1 Tbsp (15 mL) minced ginger

1 Tbsp (15 mL) finely chopped or minced lemongrass

1 Tbsp (15 mL) peanut oil

1 Tbsp (15 mL) sesame oil

1 small red chili, chopped and seeded

1 lb (450 g) ground pork

¼ cup (60 mL) lime juice

2 Tbsp (30 mL) fish sauce

1 Tbsp (15 mL) gluten-free tamari sauce

1 red onion, thinly sliced

1 cup (250 mL) fresh cilantro, chopped

¼ cup (60 mL) shredded fresh mint

Cracked black pepper to taste

2 cups (500 mL) shredded iceberg lettuce

Crushed peanuts for garnish

Lime wedges for garnish

1. Cook rice according to the instructions on the package. Set aside.

2. In a frying pan over medium heat, sauté the ginger and lemongrass in the peanut oil and sesame oil for about 2 minutes, until the ginger and lemongrass become fragrant.

3. Toss in the chili and sauté for another minute. (Use more chilies if you want more heat. You can also use dried chili flakes.)

4. Add the pork and cook until done, around 6 to 8 minutes. Remove from heat and allow to cool slightly.

5. In a large bowl, combine the pork, lime juice, fish sauce, tamari sauce, red onion, cilantro, and shredded mint. Toss well and season with cracked black pepper.

6. Serve in individual serving bowls or medium-sized plates. Line the bottom with the iceberg lettuce, add a scoop of rice, and top with the Thai-style pork.

7. Garnish with some crushed peanuts and a wedge of lime.

MAKES 4 TO 6 SERVINGS

WARM GOAT CHEESE AND PISTACHIO SALAD

Let's face it, anything with goat cheese is usually pretty delicious. This is the perfect comfort salad—the warmth of the cheese, the smoky arugula, and the sweet and tart dried cranberries. Put it out on any occasion and get ready to impress your guests.

NOTE: If you can't find a large goat cheese log, form your own from a smaller log or make one out of goat cheese from a container.

Two ½-inch (1 cm) thick rounds of goat cheese from a 2½-inch (6.5 cm) goat cheese log (about the size of a hockey puck, eh?)
½ cup (125 mL) ground pistachio nuts
4 cups (1 L) arugula
½ cup (125 mL) shredded radicchio
2 cups (500 mL) sliced pears
½ cup (125 mL) chopped walnuts + extra for garnish
¼ cup (60 mL) dried cranberries

DRESSING:
¼ cup (60 mL) walnut oil
1 Tbsp (15 mL) diced shallots
2 Tbsp (30 mL) rice wine vinegar or apple cider vinegar
2 Tbsp (30 mL) orange juice, freshly squeezed
1 tsp (5 mL) Dijon mustard
2 Tbsp (30 mL) chopped fresh parsley
Salt and cracked black pepper to taste

1. Preheat the oven to 350°F (175°C). Line a baking sheet with aluminum foil.

2. Roll the goat cheese in the ground pistachio nuts, place on the baking sheet, and bake for 6 to 8 minutes, until the edges of goat cheese start to turn golden.

3. Line a large serving platter with the arugula, radicchio, sliced pears, walnuts, and cranberries.

4. In a small bowl, whisk together the walnut oil, shallots, rice wine vinegar, orange juice, Dijon mustard, and parsley. Season with salt and cracked black pepper.

5. When the goat cheese is ready, slide it onto the greens, pour the dressing on top, add a few extra walnuts, and mix well. Or you can just drizzle with walnut oil, lemon juice, and salt and cracked black pepper.

MAKES 4 SERVINGS

PERFECTION IN A JAR

This salad secured my lifetime membership in the "Cool Moms' Club" at my daughter's school. I had the ladies over for a night under the California stars and served this as an appetizer. They are now officially friends for life. I think the salad helped . . .

4 Mason jars or 4 of your nicest medium-sized drinking glasses

3 cups (750 mL) cherry or grape tomatoes, red and yellow

1 to 2 heirloom tomatoes

1 to 2 avocados

Two 8–10 oz (225–300g) balls of burrata cheese

1 cup (250 mL) **Basil Cashew Pesto** (see p. 20)

½ cup (125 mL) toasted pine nuts (see p. 24)

Cracked black pepper to taste

Fresh basil for garnish

1. Roast the cherry (or grape) tomatoes, following the instructions in the recipe for **Roasted Cherry Tomatoes and Pancetta Pasta** (see p. 79) and set aside.

2. Slice the heirloom tomatoes and cut the avocado in half-moon wedges.

3. In the Mason jars, begin to layer the ingredients. Start with the tangy roasted tomatoes, a little bit of the fresh tomatoes, some burrata cheese, avocado, and then a dollop of the **Basil Cashew Pesto**. Keep layering until you get to the top.

4. Top each jar with toasted pine nuts, some cracked black pepper, and fresh basil. It looks and tastes beautiful.

MAKES 4 SERVINGS

NOTE: You can layer all the ingredients and store the jars in the refrigerator until you are ready to serve the salad. Then top with the pesto, pine nuts, and basil leaves.

AEGEAN DREAM WITH HONEY CROSTINI

I love Greek salads thanks to my childhood friend Wendy. We've been making them since the eighth grade. This is a twist on an old classic. I was in Greece last summer and not one restaurant served a Greek salad with lettuce—just beautiful tomatoes, onions, peppers, cucumbers, and exquisite olive oil and feta cheese. Wonderfully simple!

¾ cup (185 mL) sliced red onion
1½ cups (375 mL) seeded, chopped cucumbers
3 cups (750 mL) tomatoes, cut chunky (use heirloom tomatoes if you can get them)
½ cup (125 mL) Kalamata olives
1 cup (250 mL) chopped green pepper
1½ cups (375 mL) high-quality feta cheese
¼ cup (60 mL) chopped fresh oregano

½ cup (125 mL) chopped fresh Italian parsley
¼ cup (60 mL) olive oil (approx.)
2 Tbsp (30 mL) red wine vinegar or balsamic vinegar or **Mediterranean Madness** dressing (see p. 89)
Salt and cracked black pepper to taste
¼ cup (60 mL) toasted pine nuts (see p. 24)
Honey Crostini (recipe follows)

1. In a large bowl, combine the onion, cucumbers, tomatoes, olives, green pepper, and feta cheese. Mix well.

2. Add the oregano, parsley, olive oil, red wine vinegar or balsamic vinegar (or use the **Mediterranean Madness** dressing), salt, and lots of cracked black pepper.

3. Transfer to a large platter and garnish with pine nuts.

4. Serve with **Honey Crostini** and enjoy.

MAKES 4 SERVINGS

HONEY CROSTINI

4 pieces of gluten-free bread
2 Tbsp (30 mL) olive oil
1 tsp (5 mL) kosher salt

2 Tbsp (30 mL) honey
½ cup (125 mL) Greek yogurt
Cracked black pepper to taste

1. Preheat the oven to 350°F (175°C). Brush the bread with a little olive oil and sprinkle with kosher salt. Toast in the oven until the bread is golden brown.

2. Remove bread from the oven, spread a little honey on and a dollop of Greek yogurt. Season with cracked black pepper.

MAKES 4 CROSTINI

MAGICAL MUSTARD SALAD

Why not try...adding some shredded chicken (see p. 44) or a can of tuna and rolling it up in gluten-free wraps or rice wraps? Adding bacon or pancetta would make it even more delicious! You can also add some dates, or roasted cherry tomatoes, or some thinly sliced Black Forest ham.

Or serve on top of **Black Bean and Quinoa Burgers** (see p. 93) instead of a bun.

This is the easiest salad and everybody asks for it. Three or four ingredients—that's it!

4 to 5 cups (1 to 1.25 L) arugula
½ cup (125 mL) chopped
  walnuts
1 avocado, chopped
Shaved Parmesan cheese to
  taste (use lots!)

Dijon Mustard Lemon Swirl
  dressing to taste (see p. 13)
Salt and cracked black pepper
  to taste

1. In a large bowl, combine arugula, walnuts, avocado, and shaved Parmesan cheese. Toss well in the **Dijon Mustard Lemon Swirl** dressing and finish with cracked black pepper and salt.

MAKES 4 TO 6 SERVINGS

OMG! DID YOU SAY VEGGIES?

TABOO IN OUR HOUSE

I think vegetables are almost my favorite things. I have at times been a vegetarian but I am always lured back by a good burger or a great steak. The thing I love most about cooking is the whole process of shopping and discovering local produce and different ways of using everyday ingredients. I have visited some great markets. In St. Tropez I found the best fish market ever, and the most fragrant market has to be the Christmas market in Baja California.

Get some enjoyment out of selecting your food and what you choose to eat. Get to know your local grocer and ask for products or produce that you'd like to try. The produce store I used in Canada, The Market, in Lakefield, Ontario, is one of the best stores I have ever encountered—way better, in fact, than the high-priced grocers I have dealt with in the past. With pristine, beautiful fruits and veggies (organic and local), every time I shop there, I am excited about what I might find. They also make their own dips, salads, baked goods—everything! It is really important as you begin this journey, and sustain it, to be inspired along the way. A good grocery store can do that for you.

I know what you're thinking . . . I should get out more
(especially on Saturday night!)

RECIPES

SHITAKE MUSHROOM GINGER FRIED RICE

Everybody loves fried rice. This recipe has a punch of ginger, some great veggies, and is good on its own or paired with grilled salmon, chicken, or stir-fried beef with a little sesame oil and orange zest.

1½ cups (375 mL) uncooked rice

2 Tbsp (30 mL) chopped ginger

1 clove garlic, minced

1 cup (250 mL) sliced green onion (slice on the bias)

2 Tbsp (30 mL) sesame oil

3 cups (750 mL) shitake mushrooms, chopped

1 cup (250 mL) julienned red pepper

3 eggs whisked together

1 Tbsp (15 mL) chopped fresh chives

¼ cup (60 mL) gluten-free tamari sauce

½ cup (125 mL) fresh or frozen peas

½ cup (125 mL) cashews, chopped

¼ cup (60 mL) chopped fresh Italian parsley

1. Cook rice according to the instructions on the package and set aside.

2. In a large frying pan, sauté the ginger, garlic, and green onions in the sesame oil, until the green onions start to soften.

3. Add the shitake mushrooms and red pepper and cook for another 3 to 4 minutes, until they start to soften. Push the veggie mixture to one side of the pan.

4. On the other side of the pan, pour in the whisked eggs and scramble. Add the rice, chives, tamari sauce, and peas, mixing all the ingredients well.

5. Cook for another 2 to 3 minutes, until the peas are cooked through, then transfer to a large platter.

6. Garnish with the chopped cashews and fresh parsley.

MAKES 4 SERVINGS

BRUSSELS SPROUTS HEAVEN

Get ready to fall in love with Brussels sprouts for the first time. This salad is rich, cozy, and so flavorful. My daughter Lola cannot get enough—nor can Jack—just don't tell him he's eating Brussels sprouts! I tested it at my cottage and Lola and my mother couldn't stop eating it.

½ cup (125 mL) pancetta, diced
2 Tbsp (30 mL) olive oil
2¼ cups (560 mL) Brussels sprouts, thinly sliced lengthwise
½ lemon, juiced
3 Tbsp (45 mL) **Classic Vinaigrette** (see p. 14)
¼ cup (60 mL) pistachio nuts, chopped

1 softly poached egg (poach for about 3 to 4 minutes until the egg is cooked but the yolk is runny)
¼ cup (60 mL) shaved Pecorino Romano cheese
Salt and cracked black pepper to taste

1. In a pan, sauté the pancetta in the olive oil until crispy.

2. Add the Brussels sprouts and coat well with the oil and the pancetta. Add the lemon juice and cook until al dente, about 3 to 4 minutes—make sure sprouts have some bite in the center. Do not overcook!

3. Toss the sprouts in the **Classic Vinaigrette** with the pistachios.

4. Serve in a colorful bowl with the poached egg on top and sprinkled with the freshly shaved Pecorino Romano cheese. Break the egg yolk and toss again at the table.

5. Garnish with salt and cracked black pepper and mix well, using the poached egg as part of the dressing. Yummy!

MAKES 2 SERVINGS

THAI BASIL EGGPLANT

I love eggplant and this is a really easy way to tart up a normal weekday dinner. It is salty and sweet and super easy.

3 Asian eggplants, cut into wedges no more than 1 inch (2.5 cm) wide

2 Tbsp (30 mL) peanut oil, adding more as you go

2 Tbsp (30 mL) sesame oil

2 cloves garlic, minced

2 tsp (10 mL) chopped fresh ginger

1 small chili pepper, chopped and seeded

3 green onions, sliced on the diagonal

¼ cup (60 mL) gluten-free chicken stock

3 Tbsp (45 mL) fish sauce

1 Tbsp (15 mL) gluten-free tamari sauce

1 Tbsp (15 mL) rice vinegar

2 Tbsp (30 mL) brown sugar

1 Tbsp (15 mL) lime juice

1 tsp to 1 Tbsp (5 to 15 mL) cornstarch to thicken

1 cup (250 mL) fresh basil

¼ cup (60 mL) chopped salted peanuts, for garnish

1. In a pan over medium heat, sauté the eggplant in the peanut oil and sesame oil until soft and the skin has become chewy, about 5 to 8 minutes. You may need to add more peanut oil. Remove from pan.

2. In the same pan, add a little peanut oil and sauté the garlic, ginger, chili, and green onions until they start to soften.

3. Add the cooked eggplant and deglaze the pan with the chicken stock, cooking for another 1 to 2 minutes.

4. In a small bowl, whisk together the fish sauce, tamari sauce, rice vinegar, brown sugar, lime juice, and cornstarch.

5. Add the fish sauce mixture to the eggplant and bring to a boil. Reduce to a simmer and cook until the sauce thickens.

6. Add the basil and toss well in the pan. Garnish with chopped salted peanuts and serve immediately.

MAKES 4 SERVINGS

ASPARAGUS WITH GRAINY MUSTARD AND AVOCADO

This is a simple twist to make your asparagus experience even more decadent and rich. I've added some avocado and mustard for a savory, hearty dish that's perfect with roast pork or lemon chicken.

½ cup (125 mL) shallots, chopped
1 cup (250 mL) chopped bacon
2 Tbsp (30 mL) olive oil
4 cups (1 L) chopped asparagus, blanched and cut into 2-inch (5 cm) pieces
½ lemon, juiced

2 Tbsp (30 mL) grainy mustard
¼ cup (60 mL) chopped fresh Italian parsley
2 avocados, chopped
Toasted pine nuts for garnish (see p. 24)
Cracked black pepper for garnish

1. In a large frying pan, cook the shallots and bacon in the olive oil over medium heat until the bacon is crispy and the onions are soft.

2. Add the asparagus and lemon juice, and toss.

3. Add the mustard and parsley, and toss well. Add the avocados last minute and toss again.

4. Transfer to a serving platter and garnish with toasted pine nuts and cracked black pepper.

MAKES 4 TO 6 SERVINGS

MAPLE ROASTED VEGGIES WITH ARUGULA

Why not try…

roasting the veggies and serving them with hoisin pork? Just take **Hoisin for Days** sauce (see p. 25) and coat a pork tenderloin with it. Throw on some toasted sesame seeds and bake in a 375°F (190°F) oven for about 20 to 25 minutes, until the pink is gone. Slice and arrange on a platter with the roasted veggies.

This is the ultimate winter weather salad. I usually serve this as an appetizer that everyone can dig into together. Followed by roast chicken and green beans, it is the perfect way to celebrate the raging cold outside.

2 cups (500 mL) cubed sweet potatoes
2 cups (500 mL) cubed parsnips
1 cup (250 mL) cubed purple potatoes or halved fingerling potatoes
1 red onion, chopped
2 cups (500 mL) leeks, chopped
5 cloves garlic
¼ cup (60 mL) olive oil + extra for drizzling
2 Tbsp (30 mL) chopped fresh rosemary

3 Tbsp (45 mL) chopped fresh thyme
¼ cup (60 mL) maple syrup or honey
½ lemon, juiced
1 Tbsp (15 mL) brown sugar
2 Tbsp (30 mL) gluten-free tamari sauce
4 cups (1 L) arugula
½ cup (125 mL) crumbled blue cheese
½ cup (125 mL) pecans
½ cup (125 mL) dried cranberries
Salt and cracked black pepper to taste

1. Preheat the oven to 385°F (195°C) and line a baking sheet with aluminum foil.

2. In a large bowl, combine the sweet potatoes, parsnips, purple potatoes, red onion, leeks, and garlic.

3. In a small mixing bowl, whisk together the olive oil, rosemary, thyme, maple syrup, lemon juice, brown sugar, and tamari sauce. Pour over veggies and mix well.

4. Put the veggies on the baking sheet and roast for 50 to 60 minutes, until golden brown and cooked.

5. While the veggies are roasting, line a serving platter with the arugula.

6. When the veggies are done and still warm, spoon them over the arugula. Add the blue cheese, pecans, and dried cranberries. Drizzle with a little olive oil and garnish with salt and lots of cracked black pepper.

7. Put it in front of your guests at the table and get ready for absolute silence as they eat every last bit.

MAKES 4 SERVINGS

PISTACHIO CRUSTED CAULIFLOWER

Cauliflower is almost my favorite vegetable. I have very fond memories of Sunday night dinner with cauliflower au gratin, roast beef, and Yorkshire pudding, with my parents and all four of us siblings getting along in perfect harmony . . . sort of.

One 2 to 3 lb (900 to 1.4 kg) head of cauliflower
3 Tbsp (45 mL) olive oil
1 tsp (5 mL) kosher salt
¼ cup (60 mL) ground pistachios
½ cup (125 mL) butter

¾ cup (185 mL) gluten-free breadcrumbs
¾ cup (185 mL) Oka or Gruyère cheese, grated
2 Tbsp (30 mL) chopped fresh chives
Cracked black pepper and salt to taste

1. Preheat the oven to 375°F (190°C).

2. Lightly oil a square baking dish.

3. Core the cauliflower, leaving the head intact, and put it in the baking dish. Drizzle with the olive oil and sprinkle with kosher salt.

4. Bake for about 45 to 55 minutes until golden brown, turning over once. Remove from the oven.

5. While the cauliflower is cooking, combine in a medium size bowl the pistachios, butter, breadcrumbs, cheese, and chives. Rub together to make a crumble-like mixture.

6. Spread the breadcrumb mixture evenly over the cauliflower. Bake for 6 to 8 minutes until the cheese is runny.

7. Serve on a platter, cut into wedges, scooping up all the extra cheese and breadcrumbs.

8. Season with salt and cracked black pepper.

9. Yummy!

MAKES 10 INDIVIDUAL WEDGE SERVINGS

CAULIFLOWER AND SWEET POTATO CURRY

Why not try…serving with a watermelon and feta salad? Cube 2 to 3 cups (500 to 750 mL) watermelon, some feta cheese and shredded basil. Drizzle with a little balsamic vinegar and serve.

This is a good basic curry recipe using vegetables, but you can always add more protein—tofu, chicken, shrimp—whatever you fancy.

1 cup (250 mL) chopped onions
2 Tbsp (30 mL) olive oil
2 Tbsp (30 mL) gluten-free curry paste (or use the **Curry Paste** recipe p. 49) or powder
2 Tbsp (30 mL) fresh ginger, chopped
3 cloves garlic, chopped
4 cups (1 L) chopped sweet potatoes
3 cups (750 mL) chopped cauliflower
One 28 oz (796 mL) can of plum tomatoes
One 19 oz (540 mL) can of chickpeas, drained

2 cups (500 mL) gluten-free chicken or veggie stock
1 lime, juiced
1 cup (250 mL) chopped fresh cilantro, divided + extra for garnish
½ cup (125 mL) organic dried apricots, chopped
One 19 oz (540 mL) can coconut milk, unsweetened
2 Tbsp (30 mL) honey
¼ cup (60 mL) fresh mint, chopped
½ cup (125 mL) fresh basil, chopped
Salt and pepper to taste
Shredded coconut for garnish

1. In a large pot over medium heat, sauté the onions in olive oil until they start to soften.

2. Add the curry paste, ginger, and garlic, and cook for another 1 to 2 minutes.

3. Add the sweet potatoes and cauliflower and coat well with the curry mixture.

4. Add the plum tomatoes, chickpeas, stock, lime juice, and ½ cup (125 mL) cilantro, and cook for about 30 to 35 minutes, until the potatoes are done.

5. Then add the apricots, coconut milk, honey, and the rest of the cilantro, and cook for another 30 to 35 minutes.

6. During the last 5 minutes of cooking, add the mint and the basil, and season with salt and pepper.

7. Garnish with shredded coconut and more fresh cilantro. Serve with lots of basmati rice.

MAKES 4 TO 6 SERVINGS

SOUP TRIBUTE TO KEN KOSTICK

I dedicate this section to my late, great best friend Ken
Kostick. He was the Canadian Soup Nazi—I have never
met a person who loved soup more than Kenny! He would
purée anything and call it soup, even though sometimes it
seemed more like a smoothie to me. It didn't matter. The
pure joy he experienced when making another soup out
of almost anything, made me proud over 800 episodes
of cooking shows, and over 15 years of working together.
Lola and Jack and I tell Kenny Kostick stories on a frequent
basis, especially when we're feeling a little blue.

RECIPES

POTATO AND BRIE SOUP WITH CHIVES

I tested this recipe in the sweltering heat of July, and Lola and I still managed to have a couple of bowls each. Talk about comfort in a bowl. Most of Lola's favorite recipes in this book are soups, making a good case for introducing your kids to the magic and nutrition of a good bowl of soup.

Why not try…this soup with celeriac or parsnips? Instead of Brie you can use Camembert, Swiss, or even goat cheese. I love it with Brie!

1 cup (250 mL) chopped onions
1 cup (250 mL) chopped leeks
2 Tbsp (30 mL) olive oil
Salt and pepper to taste
1 Tbsp (15 mL) Dijon mustard
4 cups (1 L) cubed Yukon Gold potatoes
6½ to 7 cups (1.6 to 1.75 L) gluten-free chicken stock

1 Tbsp (15 mL) chopped fresh rosemary
1 cup (250 mL) Brie cheese, chopped
½ tsp (2.5 mL) ground nutmeg
½ cup (125 mL) chopped fresh chives + extra for garnish
½ cup (125 mL) milk or whipping cream (optional)
Cracked black pepper

NOTE: It's always better to leave soups a little chunky when you purée them. You can always add more stock, milk, or cream to dilute the soup.

1. In a large soup pot, sauté the onions and leeks in olive oil until they start to soften. Season with salt and pepper.

2. Add the mustard, potatoes, stock, and rosemary, and bring to a boil. Reduce to medium heat and cook for about 30 minutes, until the potatoes are done and the liquid has reduced by about 20 to 25 percent. Remove from heat and allow to cool.

3. When the soup is cool, purée in a food processor or blender.

4. Return the soup to the pot and heat it over medium-low heat.

5. Add the Brie and ground nutmeg and incorporate them into the soup. Add the chives. Season with salt and pepper if needed.

6. Taste the soup to judge the consistency. If the soup is too chunky, dilute it with a little milk or cream.

7. Garnish with cracked black pepper and more chives.

MAKES 4 SERVINGS

CHICKEN LEMONGRASS SOUP

This is a simple but exotic soup that will definitely take you outside your comfort zone. Serve as a main course for a dinner party with lots of lemon-grilled shrimp and a mango salad.

2 cups (500 mL) green onions, sliced on the bias
½ cup (125 mL) thinly sliced shallots
2 Tbsp (30 mL) sesame oil
2 Tbsp (30 mL) fresh lemongrass, finely chopped or minced
2 tsp (10 mL) chopped ginger
4 cups (1 L) gluten-free chicken stock
2 cups (500 mL) coconut milk
2 limes, juiced
1 Tbsp (15 mL) honey
3 Tbsp (45 mL) fish sauce
2 Tbsp (30 mL) gluten-free tamari sauce

½ to 1 tsp (2.5 to 5 mL) chili flakes (depending on your heat preference)
3 cups (750 mL) shredded chicken (see p. 44)
1 Tbsp (15 mL) peanut oil
1 Tbsp (15 mL) sesame seeds
3 cups (750 mL) spinach, chopped
½ cup (125 mL) chopped fresh cilantro
½ cup (125 mL) chopped fresh basil
Fresh mint for garnish
Cracked black pepper

1. In a large soup pot, sauté the green onions and shallots in sesame oil until soft.

2. Add the lemongrass and the ginger and sauté for another 2 to 3 minutes.

3. Add the stock, coconut milk, lime juice, honey, fish sauce, tamari sauce, and chili flakes, and bring to a boil.

4. Reduce to medium heat and cook for about 20 minutes, until all the flavors have blended.

5. In a frying pan, sauté the shredded chicken in the peanut oil. Coat with sesame seeds and cook for about 2 to 3 minutes to impart flavor into the shredded chicken.

6. Add the chicken, spinach, cilantro, and basil to the soup and cook for another 10 to 12 minutes until the soup thickens slightly.

7. Serve in individual bowls and garnish with a little fresh mint and cracked black pepper.

MAKES 4 SERVINGS

TORTILLA HEAVEN

This soup is a home run of flavor and nutrition. Even my father—who hates everything I cook (hence my really good therapist) loved this soup . . .

1 onion, chopped
½ cup (125 mL) chopped green onions
2 Tbsp (30 mL) olive oil
3 cloves garlic, chopped
1 medium jalapeno pepper, chopped (depending on how much heat you like)
3 cups (750 mL) shredded chicken (see p. 44)
2 cups (500 mL) cooked black beans

2 cups (500 mL) chopped tomato
6½ cups (1.6 L) gluten-free chicken stock
2 limes, juiced
1 cup (250 mL) chopped fresh cilantro, divided + extra for garnish
Salt and pepper to taste
2 cups (500 mL) shredded corn tortillas or corn chips
1 cup (250 mL) sour cream
1 to 2 avocados, diced

1. In a large soup pot, sauté the onion and green onions in olive oil until soft.

2. Add the garlic and jalapeno pepper and sauté for 1 to 2 minutes.

3. Add the chicken and coat well with the onion mixture.

4. Add the black beans, chopped tomato, stock, lime juice, and half the cilantro. Bring to a boil. Salt and pepper to taste.

5. Reduce to simmer and cook for about 30 minutes, until the soup has started to thicken. Then add the rest of the cilantro and season again.

6. Serve in individual bowls with crumbled corn tortillas or corn chips, a dollop of sour cream, and diced avocado. Add a sprig of cilantro and allow your guests to mix up all the fresh goodness.

MAKES 4 SERVINGS

PEA SOUP WITH MINT CREAM

I am going to give you two versions of this soup—one hot and one cold. It's always good to have choices. My male friends say it's good to have a "floater" or a Plan B, just in case. I don't think they were referring to soup (more along the boyfriend front), but I still think it applies . . .

¼ cup (60 mL) fresh mint, shredded
¾ cup (185 mL) sour cream
1 cup (250 mL) chopped pancetta, divided
2 Tbsp (30 mL) olive oil, divided
1 onion, chopped
Salt and pepper to taste

1 cup (250 mL) chopped leeks
½ potato, diced
4 cups (1 L) cooked peas
6 cups (1.5 L) gluten-free chicken stock
3 cups (750 mL) fresh spinach
Cracked black pepper to taste
½ cup (125 mL) goat cheese

1. Combine mint and sour cream in a small bowl and set aside.

2. In a frying pan, cook ¼ cup (60 mL) pancetta in 1 Tbsp (15 mL) olive oil over medium heat until it is crispy. Set aside for garnish.

3. In a large soup pot, sauté the rest of the pancetta, and the onion in the remaining 1 Tbsp (15 mL) olive oil. Season with salt and pepper.

4. Add the leeks and the potato and sauté for another 2 to 3 minutes.

5. Add the peas and the soup stock and bring to a boil. Simmer at medium heat for about 30 minutes, until the soup thickens and reduces by about 20 to 25 percent.

6. Add the fresh spinach and cook until incorporated.

7. Garnish with cracked black pepper.

8. Allow to cool and purée.

9. If making the **hot version**, put the soup back on the stove and add the goat cheese; stir until melted. To serve, put into a bowl with a dollop of the mint cream and some of the crispy pancetta.

10. For the **cold version**, after you purée the soup, whisk the sour cream and fresh mint mixture into the soup. Chill for about 30 minutes and then serve. You can garnish with the pancetta if you like.

MAKES 4 TO 6 SERVINGS

SWEET NOTHINGS—THE TWO BEST TREATS GOING

I am going to give you the two best recipes ever. One is a
healthy, tasty snack, and the other is a delicious, decadent
dessert. They are both from my friend Denise. I told her
to market them so she can retire in Italy, speak Italian,
and basically be fabulous. I was in Italy last summer and
I swear it is now my favorite place—the enjoyment of life
is off the charts, and those afternoon naps? Perfection!

RECIPES

THE MARKET'S GLUTEN-FREE BARS

Every summer when we go to Canada, we look forward to these delicious bars—I actually hide them so the kids don't eat them all. Age before beauty, I always say!

3 cups (750 mL) wheat-free oats
3 cups (750 mL) packed brown sugar
¼ cup (60 mL) gluten-free flour
1 tsp (5 mL) baking soda
1 tsp (5 mL) ground cinnamon
¼ tsp (1 mL) salt
½ cup (125 mL) coarsely chopped walnuts
½ cup (125 mL) dark chocolate chips
½ cup (125 mL) shredded coconut
¼ cup (60 mL) white sesame seeds
⅔ cup (160 mL) packed dried apricots
½ cup (125 mL) soft butter
½ cup (125 mL) liquid honey

1. Preheat the oven to 325°F (160°C).

2. Line a 9- × 13-inch (23 × 33 cm) baking dish with parchment paper.

3. In a large bowl, mix together all the ingredients except the apricots, butter, and honey.

4. Chop the apricots finely in a food processor. Add the butter and purée into a paste. Add this apricot mix to the dry ingredients along with the honey and mix well.

5. Scrape into the prepared baking dish and press evenly.

6. Bake for about 25 minutes, until edges are slightly dark.

7. Cool slightly, then place a sheet of parchment paper on top. Put some heavy cans or boxes on top to compress the "bars." Let cool overnight then cut into bars.

MAKES 10 TO 12 BARS

CHOCOLATE CHICKPEA CAKE

This cake is so delicious and dense you won't miss any of the flavor or substance of "real" cake. It's a wheat-free, dairy-free, extra moist chocolate cake. You can also use a 10-inch (25 cm) springform pan instead of using two 9-inch (23 cm) pans. Cook for 60 minutes and do not open that oven door!

Why not try...

serving it with crème fraîche or Greek yogurt and fresh fruit, if you don't want the icing (what's wrong with you?). Or for complete dairy-free, top with fresh fruit, a little maple syrup, and crushed pistachios.

6 eggs
6½ cups (1.6 L) canned chickpeas, drained and rinsed
2 cups (500 mL) sugar
1½ cups (375 mL) cocoa powder, divided

2 tsp (10 mL) baking powder
2 cups (500 mL) margarine or butter
1 cup (250 mL) icing sugar

1. Preheat the oven to 350°F (175°C).

2. Put the eggs, chickpeas, sugar, ½ cup (125 mL) of the cocoa powder, and the baking powder in a food processor and blend until smooth.

3. Pour into two 9-inch (23 cm) round cake pans. Bake for 60 minutes.

4. While the cake is baking, blend the margarine (or butter), icing sugar, and the remaining 1 cup (250 mL) cocoa powder in the food processor until smooth.

5. Allow the cakes to cool, then stack them and slather with icing.

MAKES TWO 9-INCH (23 CM) CAKES

ACKNOWLEDGEMENTS

This book, of all the things I have done, has been the most personal—even more than my book on divorce. In the fog of a health scare and events that dramatically changed my life (and I have had a few) I wanted to turn the experience around, to learn and grow from it, and maybe make a difference in someone else's life.

First and foremost I would like to thank Lola Elizabeth Eustace for being the powerhouse that she is and the most resilient, magical person I know—one interaction with her and you are hooked. Her outer beauty is only surpassed by her spirit and love of life. She has taught me a thing or two about waking up each day grateful and ready to go. When she looks at me with those big brown eyes, I almost forget she has just tormented the dogs for two hours or locked Jack in his room. I prefer to think of her as feisty.

Another major shout out goes to my "mini me"—not so mini anymore at six-foot-four—my son Jack Montgomery McDermott. Nobody makes me laugh harder than Jack; he is the most positive person I know. When Lola was losing her hair, he proclaimed, "Who cares?" and vowed to shave his head for her in solidarity! "It's only hair" he said. "What's the big deal? Plus, have you looked at Mom's hair lately? That's really bad news!"

Also on the list is my beautiful mother Maureen, for always being an inspiration. And my wonderful friends who have supported me through every major crisis and opportunity—Anne and Chris, specifically—who treat me with the complete lack of respect I deserve! My California posse and their kids—Teresa, Jackson, Stephanie, Kiernan, and Schuyler—were a good group of guinea pigs for my food.

I am fortunate to have the most amazing support system of phenomenal women: Julie Hewett, the creative genius behind "Julie Hewett Cosmetics," who has been a devoted friend and inspiration for over 10 years—she is the ultimate California girl, born and bred, and famous worldwide for her gorgeous products and impressive film resume; Jennifer Burton, a lifesaver and single mom extraordinaire, brilliant at helping people navigate their path; my partner in crime— one of the sweetest, most joyful friends ever, Miss Adriane; and finally, Debbie Robins—I don't know how I found you, but within weeks you had opened every door that I had closed and showed me the possibility and power of being authentic and true to the call to service. You are absolutely one of a kind.

I owe another huge heap of gratitude to Amy Gibson of Creative Hair in Los Angeles. She is a force to be reckoned with. Diagnosed with alopecia at the age of 13, she lost all her hair, went on to become an Emmy-nominated actress with a career that spanned decades, and hid her condition for years. But then she decided to share her experience, forming a company that helps women and men with all kinds of hair loss—from autoimmune disease to cancer and everything in between. The day I dreaded more than anything—shopping for a wig or hairpiece for my daughter—turned into one of the most magical days ever, thanks to Amy. She immediately put Lola and me at ease, throwing wigs and hair accessories around like a crazy woman! Her expertise is hard won; she has lived the part, so her empathy and experience are priceless. Within minutes, we had found the perfect, most beautiful piece for Lola, and I knew no matter what happened, we were covered. Lola put it on and said the best thing ever: "This just feels like me." Thanks, Amy!

Also on the list is Lola's school, St. Francis de Sales in Sherman Oaks, especially her third grade teacher Mr. Warren Wileman, who gave her a magical year and me tons of support, and Ms. Rebbe, who is continuing the support in Grade 4. Plus, of course, her great doctor, Christopher Ho, who has been invaluable in getting Lola the best treatments and care possible.

I was also lucky enough to have two fantastic food sponsors for the book, who covered all the bases on the key to cooking and eating well. In the United States I secured Sprouts Farmer's Market to help with the food, and in Canada a local boutique grocer called The Market came on board. I used them both for different reasons.

I am in love with Sprouts—the quality, the price, the people who work in the stores. Every time I go there, I discover some great new product that I love, that's reasonably priced and unique. Who would have thought that cooking gluten-free could be economical! When we think of health food, especially gluten-free, we think it involves big dollars. And that in itself is a big deterrent. I had many conversations with them about the importance of great, affordable healthy food, and how crucial it is for people to have access to quality without being financially penalized. It was a complete pleasure working with them. It is what great food shopping should be—everything from their in-house oils and products to their beauty and vitamin sections—easy, fun, and informative.

Also close to my heart is The Market in Lakefield, Ontario, owned by Denise and Lee, one of the most happily married couples I know. They just expanded their store and it is packed with the most delicious produce and products—field tomatoes, peaches-and-cream corn, new potatoes, gourmet cheeses, and lots of gluten-free treats. I love shopping there because they are my local grocer and know what I am looking for and what I like. Lee always puts away perfectly ripe avocados for me, and heaps of basil, because he knows I love them both. They know their customers personally, so every time you shop, they can tell you what is the freshest and what you should try. It is really important to have a major retailer you can trust, and a local or neighborhood store to cover all your shopping needs. Together they are the perfect combination.

And last, but not least, to my best friend Ken Kostick, whom I had the pleasure (and the pain) of working with for over 15 years. It was the best of times and the best job ever, with over 800 episodes of cooking shows and two years of hosting a morning radio show called *What's for Breakfast?* I have never laughed harder with anyone, anytime, anywhere. He was kind, complicated, hysterically crazy and funny, and one of my favorite people, hands down. Miss and love you every day…

Signed,

"The Big Girl"

INDEX